know your
Poisonous Plants

poisonous plants found in field and garden

Photographs by
    J. Carroll Reiners

Photographs by
  J. Carroll Reiners

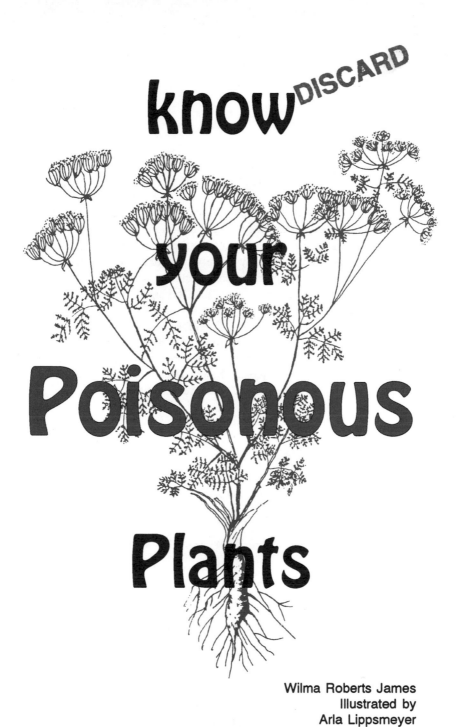

know DISCARD
your
Poisonous
Plants

Wilma Roberts James
Illustrated by
Arla Lippsmeyer

Naturegraph Publishers

ACKNOWLEDGMENTS

The author wishes to extend her gratitude to Arla Lippsmeyer for her united endeavor in producing the illustrations for the many descriptions used in this book. Credit should certainly be given to the librarians of the Sacramento City, County Library who kindly and patiently helped search for much needed reference material, as well as to the many authors listed in the references whose painstaking work was an invaluable aid. Appreciation is expressed for the use of the color photographs on page 2 and 3 by J. Carroll Reiners, a member of the Photographic Society of America, accredited nature and pictorial photographer, lecturer, and judge. The scenic cover picture showing the flowering lupine was photographed by Gene Ahrens. The oleander was photographed by J. Gregory Twain who also designed the cover and title page.

ISBN 0-87961-012-3

Library of Congress Catalog Card Number: 73-13884

Copyright © Wilma Roberts James 1973

2000 printing

Naturegraph Publishers has been publishing books on natural history, Native Americans, and outdoor subjects since 1946. Please write for our free catalog.

Naturegraph Publishers, Inc.
3543 Indian Creek Road
Happy Camp, CA 96039
(530) 493-5353

Books for a better world

TABLE OF CONTENTS

INTRODUCTION

People have always lived near plants that can cause a skin rash, an illness or death. Through the years, many of these plants have been brought into home gardens and public parks from their natural surroundings. More than likely you have plants containing poison growing in or around the outside of your home since they grow wild in vacant lots, in swamps, in dry fields, in the deep woods and in open meadows.

Some of our most poisonous plants are used in making valuable medicines. Often life-saving drugs come from the most beautiful of plants. A good example is the common purple foxglove grown in gardens and happily-discovered growing in shady woods. The digitalis taken from its leaves and seeds strengthens the heartbeat of an ill person, but unless a doctor prescribes the proper amount the results of incorrect dosage can be fatal.

Poisonous plants are found among our most prized trees, shrubs, vegetables and vines. They give us shade, colorful flowers, and food. We look forward to seeing the wild flowers of spring many of which are common weeds containing toxic compounds. On the other hand the popular and widely planted English ivy is an example of a poisonous vine that creates a cool and inviting atmosphere on a hot summer day.

Because such a large number of poisonous plants are so useful in one way or another, no doubt they will continue to be cultivated and enjoyed. **However, everyone should be aware of their danger.** There are more than 500 known species of poisonous plants growing in the United States but luckily only a few are dangerously poisonous. The greatest number are less harmful if not eaten in large quantities. Some of the least poisonous plants can be the most irritating to the skin if touched.

The best treatment for plant poisoning is to not let it happen. This book tells about the most common plants to avoid. If you learn their names, where they grow, and what they look like, you can protect yourself and your family against the worst of the trouble makers.

WHAT TO DO ABOUT PLANT POISONING

Accidents will happen even though we try to be careful. Phone your doctor at once if there is any reason to believe you or someone else has been poisoned by a plant. Remember the signs of poisoning may not appear for as long as 6 to 15 hours after tasting, chewing or swallowing.

Your doctor will want to know all about the plant that caused the illness. If you cannot recall the name of the plant, tell the doctor what it looks like. Make clear to him everything that was eaten during the last fifteen hours.

Everything the doctor learns over the telephone will help him decide the cause of the poisoning. It will help him determine the proper treatment for the trouble. Your doctor may explain how to care for the ill person at home if the poisoning is not too serious.

What can you do if your doctor is not in his office? The next thing is to call your nearest **Poison Control Center.** Doctors have set up about six hundred of these centers in cities across the United States.

Poison Control Centers are usually in hospitals. They are ready to take calls all hours of the day or night. A telephone operator will help you call the center if you do not know where it is located.

The Poison Control Center can advise you as to whether or not the plant was poisonous. Whoever answers will tell you what to do until your doctor is found. You will be told if the poisoned person should be brought to the hospital without delay.

If the center says to come to the hospital right away, ask for the quickest way to get there. **Take along a sample of the poisonous plant if at all possible.** The sample can be a great aid to the doctor in charge.

FIRST AID TREATMENT

- **A conscious person may be given a tablespoon of salt in a glass of warm water to bring on vomiting.**
- **An unconscious person should receive artificial respiration only.**
- **Keep the patient warm and quiet.**
- **Stay close to the patient until help arrives.**

PREVENTING PLANT POISONING

The increasing number of poisonings each year would be drastically reduced if the following steps were taken. They might save you or your child's life.

1. Know which of your garden and house plants are poisonous.
2. Identify each plant before placing it in your home or yard.
3. Store bulbs and seeds where children cannot reach them.
4. Teach children to never put plants or plant parts in their mouths which are not commonly used as food.
5. Remember children are usually much more susceptible to the effects of a poison than adults.
6. Do not assume a plant is non-toxic because birds or other wildlife consume it without harm.
7. Watch small children at play. Toddlers are apt to sample anything.
8. Never eat native plants unless positive of their identification, or even use unknown twigs for various reasons (for example, a stick to roast hotdogs).
9. Do not rely upon cooking to destroy toxic substances.
10. Be aware that all people do not receive the same reaction to plants known to be poisonous on contact.
11. Avoid plants sprayed with insecticides or herbicides. These toxic substances cause moderate to severe internal poisoning. However, be aware that many people unknowingly put the blame on an insecticide when the culprit may be the plant itself.
12. Be prepared for an emergency by keeping an ounce or more of syrup of ipecac handy. It will induce vomiting and eliminate part of the poison. Vomiting can also be induced by using plenty of water with soapsuds (not a detergent), salt, baking soda, raw eggs, milk, or just lukewarm water and dilute the poison at the same time. Tickling the back of the throat after the stomach is full sometimes helps to induce vomiting. IMMEDIATE ACTION can be accomplished if you use simple measures always at hand thus removing the poison from the stomach before it can be absorbed. Check with a physician regardless.

COMMON/SCIENTIFIC FAMILIES

On the description pages, 12 through 91, COMMON FAMILY names are noted. For the reader's convenience in locating reference material these Common family names are listed alphabetically below along with their scientific counterparts.

Agave/*Agavaceae*
Amaryllis/*Amaryllidaceae*
Arum/*Araceae*
Barberry/*Berberidaceae*
Beech/*Fagaceae*
Boxwood/*Buxaceae*
Buckeye/*Hippocastanaceae*
Buckwheat/*Polygonaceae*
Carrot/*Umbelliferae*
Crowfoot/*Ranunculaceae*
Custard-Apple/*Annonaceae*
Dogbane/*Apocynaceae*
Fern/*Polypodiaceae*
Figwort/*Scrophulariaceae*
Flax/*Linaceae*
Four-O'Clock/*Nyctaginaceae*
Fumitory/*Fumariaceae*
Ginkgo/*Ginkgoaceae*
Ginseng/*Araliaceae*
Goosefoot/*Chenopodiaceae*
Gourd/*Cucurbitaceae*
Grape/*Vitaceae*
Grass/*Cramincac*
Heath/*Ericaceae*
Holly/*Aquifoliaceae*
Honeysuckle/*Caprifoliaceae*
Horsetail/*Equisetaceae*
Iris/*Iridaceae*
Lily/*Liliaceae*
Lobelia/*Lobeliaceae*
Logania/*Loganiaceae*
Madder/*Rubiaceae*

Mahogany/*Meliaceae*
Mezereon/*Thymelaeaceae*
Milkweed/*Asclepiadaceae*
Mistletoe/*Loranthaceae*
Moonseed/*Menispermaceae*
Morning-glory/*Convolvulaceae*
Mulberry/*Moraceae*
Mushroom/*Agaricaceae*
Mustard/*Cruciferae*
Nettle/*Urticaceae*
Nightshade/*Solanaceae*
Olive/*Oleaceae*
Orchid/*Orchidaceae*
Pea/*Leguminosae*
Pink/*Caryophyllaceae*
Pokeweed/*Phytolaccaceae*
Poppy/*Papaveraceae*
Primrose/*Primulaceae*
Rose/*Rosaceae*
St. Johns-wort/*Hypericaceae*
Saxifrage/*Saxifragaceae*
Soapberry/*Sapindaceae*
Spurge/*Euphorbiaceae*
Staff-tree/*Celastraceae*
Stonecrop/*Crassulaceae*
Sumac/*Anacardiaceae*
Sunflower/*Compositae*
Tobira/*Pittosporaceae*
Trumpet-creeper/*Bignoniaceae*
Vervain/*Verbenaceae*
Walnut/*Juglandaceae*
Yew/*Taxaceae*

Reader Please Note:

Abbreviation spp. means more than one species of a genus. The most poisonous parts are listed separately on pages 12-76 by the illustration using this symbol ☠

ANGEL'S TRUMPET, *Datura suaveolens*
(Nightshade Family)

This ornamental, 10-15 foot high shrub is raised in gardens and greenhouses for its huge, sweet musk-scented, trumpet-shaped, white flowers that open at night. It is planted permanently outdoors in frost-free areas of California and Florida. Elsewhere the roots are carried over winter in cellars. The chemicals within the leaves and seeds of the evergreen plant have been useful in medicine, but poisoning from eating parts of the plant is not uncommon. A *"tea"* made from the big, oblong, dull-green leaves (up to 1 foot and longer) accounts for many poisonings. Sucking the juice from the tubes of the flowers, as a child might do, is also dangerous. The plant does not form fruit in the southeastern part of the United States, but where it does, eating only a small amount of the black seeds found inside the spindle-shaped fruit produces symptoms of poisoning that can be fatal. (Native of Brazil)

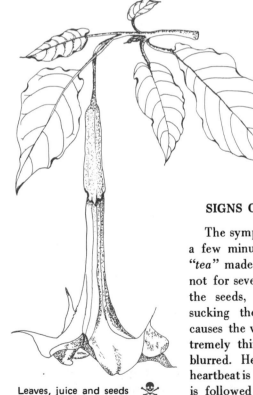

Leaves, juice and seeds ☠

SIGNS OF POISONING

The symptoms may appear in a few minutes after drinking a *"tea"* made from the plant, but not for several hours after eating the seeds, uncooked leaves or sucking the juice. Poisoning causes the victim to become extremely thirsty and his sight is blurred. He has a high fever; his heartbeat is rapid and weak. This is followed by convulsions and coma.

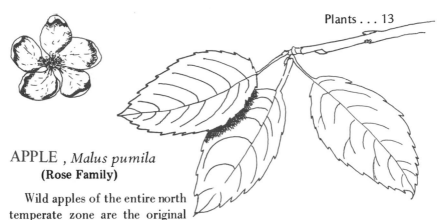

APPLE , *Malus pumila*
(Rose Family)

Wild apples of the entire north
temperate zone are the original
producers of our marketable fruit and have been cultivated from ancient
times. Today there are several hundred named varieties of the common .
apple grown in orchards and gardens throughout the United States, adapt-
ing to every type of soil. The tree is round-headed, short-trunked, and
grows to 45 feet in height. The young branches are downy. The deciduous, alternate leaves are simple, 1½-4 inches long, elliptical or ovalish,
pointed at the tip, glossy above, downy beneath, and bluntly-toothed.
The flowers, 2 inches across, are white and pink, appearing usually before the foliage. The nearly-round, solid fruit may be yellow, red, green,
or striped. All varieties of apples contain cyanide, but the black seeds
inside the core have the greatest amount of this poisonous substance.
**Deaths are on record from eating large quantities of the seeds. The
seeds should be removed** before consuming the otherwise edible fruit.
Seeds of the commonly cultivated crabapple (*M. baccata*) and its many
varieties are equally as toxic. The fruit, ¾ inches or less in diameter, is
yellow or red, tart-tasting, and safe to eat raw or cooked. (Natives of
Europe and Asia)

Seeds in quantity ☠

SIGNS OF POISONING

Symptoms of apple seed poisoning consist of vomiting, dizziness,
staggering, difficulty in breathing, weakness, spasms, coma, and death.

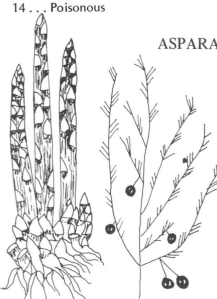

ASPARAGUS, *Asparagus officinalis*
(Lily Family)

The common perennial asparagus is grown in every part of the United States, except in regions of extreme heat. California and New Jersey lead all other states in commercial production, but many home gardeners make their own plantings. Asparagus has escaped and become naturalized everywhere. It is the most permanent of all vegetables. Once established, it will last a lifetime. Since Greek and Roman times the tender young shoots have been used for food. The young shoots begin to push up from the roots or *"crowns"* in the spring. Their leaves are reduced to scales, with usually a purple-colored bud at the tip. **Eating the green young shoots raw often causes dermatitis.** During the summer the plant develops a tall, bushy, feathery foliage that is sometimes used decoratively in homes. This space-consuming foliage is stiffish with shining, not-true leaves. Children should be warned against eating the round, scarlet berries that form on the leaf-like branchlets. (Native of the north temperate zone of the Old World)

Uncooked shoots and berries ☠

SIGNS OF POISONING

The degree of poisoning may vary from a mildly reddened skin to a most painful swelling accompanied with blisters and itchiness. The severity depends upon the amount eaten, and the sensitivity of the individual.

AUTUMN CROCUS , *Colchicum autumnale*
(Lily Family)

This crocus-like, bulbous herb is a popular garden or indoor plant grown everywhere in the United States. It has become naturalized in some areas. The leaves arising in the spring from the ground, or in a dish on a window sill, are 8-10 inches long and about 1½ inches wide. If planted outdoors, this crocus remains leafless in the summer. Unlike the spring crocus, the flowers appear in the fall. The flower clusters are 3-4 inches wide, long-tubed, lavender-purple, rose-purple, or white. The fruit is a 3-valved capsule, usually maturing with the leaves in the spring. A powerful poisonous alkaloid called colchicine, is found in every part of the plant. The bulbs are especially dangerous when ingested. Children have been poisoned by eating the flowers, leaves and seeds. Poisoning has occurred after using milk from cows that ate hay containing the leaves of the autumn crocus. The dried corms and seeds have been long used in medicine. (Native of Europe and North Africa)

All parts ☠

SIGNS OF POISONING

Eating any part of the plant will be followed by a burning sensation in the mouth, severe intestinal cramps, diarrhea, weakness, a fleeting pulse, inadequate blood pressure, and kidney failure. Death occurs due to shock and inability to obtain sufficient air in the lungs.

BELLADONNA LILY , *Amaryllis Belladonna*
(Amaryllis Family)

A perennial herb, the common garden amaryllis is grown permanently outdoors in California and Florida, but most other places the large tuberous bulbs are taken up and stored during the winter. Where the plant remains outdoors the year around, the strap-like leaves appear in the winter in clumps 2-3 feet across. It is leafless in the late spring and early summer. In August, clusters of 3-12 trumpet-shaped flowers bloom on top of the bare, reddish-brown stalks that are 2-3 feet tall. The large showy, sweet-scented flowers are typically rosy-pink, about 3½ inches long. The tube is short, with six equal divisions of the flower-cup. The fruit is a globe-shaped pod which bursts irregularly, revealing a few pellet-like seeds. *Hippeastrum* is the hybrid amaryllis, usually grown in pots, either indoors by a sunny window, or else placed in a sheltered outdoor area. There are many named varieties and the colors range from red, pink, white, salmon, to variously marked or striped kinds. (Native of South Africa)

Bulbs ☠

SIGNS OF POISONING

The alkaloids present in the bitter-tasting bulb will cause the poisoned person to tremble and vomit. This will be followed by a general feeling of weakness and too rapid a heartbeat. The pupils of the eye will become dilated. This last symptom may remain after all other signs have disappeared.

BITTERSWEET , *Celastrus scandens*
(Staff Tree Family)

American bittersweet is a deciduous, woody, climbing or trailing vine with rope-like branches. It is commonly found along roadsides, streams, in woodlands, and on old stone walls from Quebec south to North Carolina throughout the mountains, and west to the Dakotas, Kansas, Oklahoma, and New Mexico. The rampant-growing vine, from 10-20 feet high, adapts itself best where winters are cold, but along with several other species, it is often cultivated in gardens elsewhere as an ornamental. The smooth, light-green, finely-toothed, alternate, leaves are stalked, oblong-oval, 2½-5 inches long, and pointed at the tip. The clusters of greenish-white flowers and later the fruit are held above the leaves. Male and female flowers appear on different plants. In September the flowers are followed by globular orange fruit, the shell of which splits open into 3 parts and bends backward to display the brilliant red-coated seed covering. Often the fruit-bearing branches are picked, brought indoors, and used for fall and winter arrangements. Leaves, seeds, and roots contain a poisonous principle, and any species can be expected to prove toxic when eaten. (Native of eastern North America)

Leaves, seeds and roots ☠

SIGNS OF POISONING

Poisoning may cause vomiting, diarrhea, chills, weakness, convulsions, and coma.

BLACK LOCUST, *Robinia Pseudo-acacia*
(Pea Family)

All parts ☠

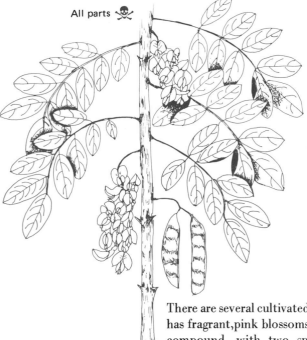

The black locust is a deeply furrowed, brown-barked, deciduous tree to 80 feet tall, and is also called yellow locust and false acacia. It is common in dry woods and along roadsides in the eastern United States and is a native of the central states. Emigrants brought seeds with them from the east, and now the tree is found everywhere in the West, often as a street tree. There are several cultivated species, one of which has fragrant, pink blossoms. Alternate leaves are compound, with two spines resembling rose thorns at the base of each leafstock. The 7-19, opposite, ovalish, smooth-margined leaflets are 1-2 inches long. The sweet-scented, white flowers, ½-¾ inches long, hang in dense drooping, 4-8 inch long clusters. After the pea-like flowers fade, the 3-4 inch long, bean-like pods form, turn brown, and may remain on the tree all winter. Poisoning has occurred after eating the seeds, leaves, young shoots, and the inner bark. Children have been poisoned by sucking on the young twigs. (Native of North and Central America)

SIGNS OF POISONING

Symptoms appear within a few hours after consuming the poisonous parts of the tree. Vomiting, diarrhea, stupor, depression, coldness of the arms and legs (and perhaps paralysis) irregular heart contractions, weak pulse and enlarged eye pupils are all noticeable. In extremely serious cases, death takes place within two or three days.

BLEEDING HEART, *Dicentra spectabilis*
(Fumitory Family)

This perennial herb from 2-3 feet high was first introduced into English gardens in the late 1700's and has long been a favorite garden ornamental in the United States. It is the showiest of all species of the bleeding heart. Western bleeding heart *(D. formosa)* is a native to the moist, shady woods along the Pacific coast. It has clusters of pale to deep-rose flowers on leafless, reddish stems, or rarely white or cream-colored flowers with rosy-tipped petals. Other native species appear in eastern North America. All species have graceful fern-like foliage, with much-dissected, basal leaves and ultimate segments deeply-lobed and narrow. These dainty, heart-shaped flowers, that appear in early spring, have short, rounded spurs and grow in a one-sided cluster that ends at the top of the stem. The foliage dies down in winter. The fruit is a slender, two-valved pod, minutely crested. The underground rootstock is branching and fleshy. The alkaloids present in all species make all parts of the plant toxic, but especially the soft, green or blue-green leaves, and the thick clump of roots. Any part of the various species may cause skin irritation on contact. (Native of Japan and North America)

All parts

SIGNS OF POISONING

Nervous symptoms are trembling, loss of balance, staggering, weakness, difficulty in breathing, and convulsions.

BUTTERCUP, *Ranunculus acris*
(Crowfoot Family)

A perennial herb, this common buttercup of moist fields, pastures, and meadows has become naturalized throughout the United States. It is weedy in the wild state, but often double-flowered in cultivated garden forms. The root is fibrous; the 2-2½ foot high green stem branched and hairy. The deep green leaves are divided into three segments and again three times cut or divided. The nearly 1 inch wide flowers are light-golden yellow inside, and light yellow on the outside with the five wide petals overlapping. They sometimes bloom from spring until frost and form fruit of a tiny cluster of dry achenes. The plant contains a bitter-tasting oil, and has from ancient times been known to be poisonous if eaten. Contact with the leaves is a common cause of dermatitis. The American Indians considered the seeds harmless and used them for food. (Native of Europe and Siberia)

All parts, except seeds ☠

SIGNS OF POISONING

Consuming any part of the plant except the seeds produces blisters or inflammation around the mouth, irritated skin, stomach pains, vomiting, diarrhea, and jerking spasms. Irritant juices may severely injure the digestive system. Other symptoms may be temporary blindness and convulsions.

CALADIUM , *Caladium spp.*
(Arum Family)

There are 12-14 species of this genus of foliage plants, all cultivated for their beautifully colored leaves. They are used extensively as ornamentals either inside the house or else as summer bedding plants. This tuberous-rooted perennial grows from 2-4 feet in height. Leaves are thin and almost translucent, with a stalk that is joined to, or near the middle of the leaf-blade. The large, smooth-margined leaves are arrowhead shaped and variously-colored with bands and blotches of white, silver, red, pink, rose and green, or rarely all green. The flowers are white and produce a berry-like fruit. Every species of caladium has a bitter poisonous juice which contains calcium oxalate crystals. These crystals are present throughout the plants and when ingested, they cause the mouth to be severely irritated. (Natives of tropical America)

All parts ☠

SIGNS OF POISONING

Soon after eating a small amount of the leaves the mouth will burn and swell. There will be an intense burning inside the throat along with a disturbed stomach, vomiting, and diarrhea. After the tongue and throat swell, breathing may become difficult. Due to the blocking of the air passage, death may occur.

CASTOR-OIL PLANT , *Ricinus communis*
(Spurge Family)

Seeds, foliage, young seedlings ☠

This striking annual shrub-like plant grows throughout the United States as an ornamental in yards and in some areas of California it is cultivated as an agricultural crop for the oil expressed from the seeds. It is not uncommon to see it growing along roads and streambeds where it has escaped. The branched, green to reddish or purple stems grow from 4-15 feet tall. Leaves are alternate, long-stalked, to 3 feet wide, with 5-11 lobes which have saw-toothed margins. Flowers appear in a dense, terminal cluster from 1-2 feet high. The fruit is a spiny pod containing the glossy, beautifully-mottled but poisonous ½-¾ inch seeds. The foliage of young seedlings is also toxic. However, the greatest amount of poison is found in the fleshy part of the mature seeds. Castor bean should never be planted in an area where small children play. As few as six seeds can cause the death of an adult, while eating two or three seeds can cause the death of a child. There is little danger if the hard-coated seeds are swallowed whole. Death from the seeds can be eliminated if the seed heads on the plant are clipped off and destroyed before they mature. Handling the leaves and seeds of the many varieties of this plant can result in serious allergies in some individuals. (Native of tropical Africa) Sometimes listed under Castor Bean.

SIGNS OF POISONING

Chewing the seeds will cause burning in the mouth, throat, and stomach. Other symptoms are vomiting, severe stomach pains, diarrhea, thirst, blurred vision, sweating, trembling, weakness, convulsions, and may be fatal.

CHINABERRY, China Tree , *Melia Azedarach*
(Mahogany Family)

The chinaberry is a deciduous, spreading tree growing to 50 feet high, which has become naturalized along edges of woods, roadsides, and in pastures in the southern United States. It is widely cultivated as an ornamental in warm areas. Texas umbrella tree, var. *umbraculiformis* is a common planted variety. The 1-3 inch long alternate leaves are compound, oval, the toothed leaflets arranged feather-fashion. Fragrant lilac or purple flowers, about 1 inch across, are in compound, loose terminal clusters. Nearly round fruit, about ¾ inch in diameter turns from green to yellowish as it matures and contains a wrinkled or strongly-ribbed stone. The fruit hangs on the tree long after the leaves fall. The furrowed, gray bark and the flowers are poisonous when eaten, but the bony, berry-like fruits and the leaves contain the greatest amount of poison. Children have been poisoned from drinking a *"tea"* made from the leaves, although poisoning from the fruit is most frequent. The outer covering of the root has been used medicinally. (Native of southern Asia)

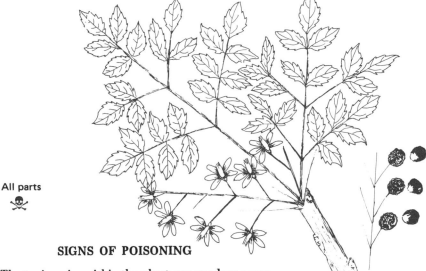

All parts

SIGNS OF POISONING

The toxic resins within the plant can produce symptoms in less than an hour or they may not appear for several hours after ingesting. There is nausea, vomiting, constipation, or diarrhea, with blood. In addition are nervous symptoms such as elation or depression, irregular breathing, mental confusion, stupor and coma. Death may occur in 24 hours.

CHRISTMAS ROSE , *Helleborus niger*
(Crowfoot Family)

This perennial herb is commonly cultivated in gardens for its mid-winter bloom. Because it blooms in early spring in some regions, the plant is often incorrectly called the Lenten rose. The evergreen basal leaves are compoundly divided into 7-9 oblong large-toothed leaflets. The flower stocks, arising from the branches of the rootstock, have a loose bract at the base and terminate in a single flower with two bracts, from which a second flower may develop. The white or pinkish-green flowers, about 2 inches wide become purplish with age. The dry, one-chambered fruit, splits along one seam. The thick but fiberous rootstock which is blackish-brown externally, yields drugs for commercial use. However, the rootstock is violently poisonous if eaten. As a warning it emits an unpleasant odor when cut or broken, and has a bitter, slightly acrid taste. The poisonous leaves may cause dermatitis on contact. (Native of Europe and western Asia)

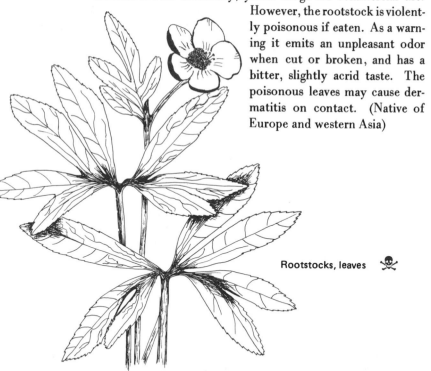

Rootstocks, leaves

SIGNS OF POISONING

Merely nibbling on the leaves or rootstock will make the mouth burn. The plant contains purgative principles which will cause stomach pains, diarrhea, and nausea. Nervous effects may also develop. Death results if the rootstock is eaten in quantities.

DAPHNE , *Daphne Mezereum*
(Mezereon Family)

This species of daphne, a deciduous woody shrub 1-4 feet high, is much cultivated as an ornamental but has escaped in the northeastern United States where it grows side by side with wild plants. Other species and hybrids are widely cultivated as ornamentals. The thin ovalish 2-3 inch long, alternate leaves are wedge-shaped at the base and without marginal teeth. The fragrant, lilac-purple or rosy-purple flowers grow in stalkless clusters of three; bloom before the leaves come out; and are ½ inch or less long. The one-seeded, round fruit, about ¼ inch in diameter, is leathery and scarlet-colored. A white variety (var. *alba)* has yellow one-seeded fruit. All parts of all species of daphnes are poisonous, but **especially the attractive fruit.** The poison is not destroyed even after the leaves and fruit wither. Eating only a few berries can be fatal to a child. It is one of the oldest plants recognized as poisonous. (Native of Eurasia)

Bark, leaves, especially fruit ☠

SIGNS OF POISONING

A glycoside present in the plant causes burning of the mouth, throat, and stomach. This is followed by vomiting, internal bleeding with bloody diarrhea, weakness, stupor, convulsions, kidney damage, coma, and death. Rubbing the leaves against the skin may produce blisters and irritation.

DEADLY AMANITA, Death Angel
Amanita phalloides, (Fungi Family)

This poisonous species of mushroom (toadstool) is common on lawns, in shaded wooded areas, and on the edges of clearings throughout most of the United States. It appears with its other deadly relatives among harmless species from June to September. *Amanita phalloides* has a cap 2-5 inches across and 4-8 inch high stem. The greenish-tinged cap later changes to a grayish-tan with a white spot in the center. White gills also distinguish it along with a cup at the base of the stem (which is the remnant of a sheath the mushroom breaks through). Sometimes it has a ring near the top of the stem, or else the cup or ring may be missing. *A. muscaria* has a surface flecked with white scales or spots. The color is pure white or pale yellow, or the cap may be yellow to brown and varying to red. The gills are white, whereas in an edible mushroom the gills are brown or purple-brown when fully developed. Eating one or two bites of these mushrooms can be fatal. Children should be warned **"Do not even touch".** Cooking does not destroy the poison nor does mixing with harmless species. (Native of North America)

All parts ☠

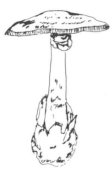

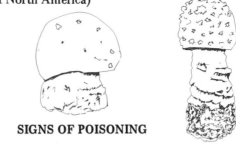

SIGNS OF POISONING

Ordinarily symptoms of amanita mushroom poisoning do not appear until 6-24 hours have passed. Then the severe stomach cramps, vomiting and diarrhea start. Strength rapidly disappears. The skin turns yellow due to liver damage. Wheezing develops, along with inadequate circulation, coma, and death. The degree of poisoning depends upon the amount eaten. Since there is no absolute safe rule in selecting edible wild mushrooms, only experts should gather them.

DEATH CAMAS , *Zigadenus venenosus*
(Lily Family)

This bulbous perennial plant is found below 8,200 feet in meadows, pastures, open slopes, and along roadsides from Canada south to Florida, Texas, New Mexico, Arizona, and California. It is also sometimes cultivated in gardens. Leaves are long, narrow and grass-like and gathered around the base of the stem. The tall stem is topped with a branched cluster of greenish-white to yellow-white 1/8-3/8 inch long flowers. The fruit is a dry capsule with three inner compartments, each containing several seeds. The onion-like bulb has a dark-colored outer coat, but lacks the onion odor. All parts of the plant are toxic, particularly the leaves and the bulb. Poisoning has followed eating of the flowers. There are 15 species of *Zigadenus* and they vary greatly in the quantity of poison contained. *Z. venenosus* has an especially high content of alkaloids and ranks as one of the most poisonous plants in the western United States. (Native of North America)

All parts ☠

SIGNS OF POISONING

Symptoms appear from 1½ hours to 8 hours after eating parts of the plant. They consist of abdominal pains, nausea, vomiting, trembling, muscular weakness, struggling for breath, lowered body temperature, coma and death.

DELPHINIUM, Larkspur , *Delphinium spp.*
(Crowfoot Family)

The annual larkspurs and the perennial delphiniums comprise a genus of over 250 species of herbs from 2-6 feet tall. This includes those planted in gardens. More than 80 native species grow in woodlands and on rocky slopes and ranges throughout the United States, but are most common in the West. A widely-cultivated European species has also escaped to roadsides and fields. Leaves are lobed or divided finger-fashion and on long stalks. Flowers are usually in a long terminal cluster, on stems to several feet tall, but shorter in annuals. The prevailing color, of the flower, is blue, while cultivated forms boast of other colors as well as double blooms. Each flower has a spur projecting backward from the upper part. The fruit is generally a many-seeded follicle. All species of the plant contain alkaloids of varying quantities. Ingesting young leaves before the flowers appear is a frequent cause of poisoning. Toxicity decreases as the plants age. Later in the season poisoning comes from eating the small seeds which hold the toxic alkaloids in concentrated amounts. Leaves and seeds may cause dermatitis on contact. These extremely dangerous plants should always be cultivated out of the reach of small children. (Native of the north temperate zone)

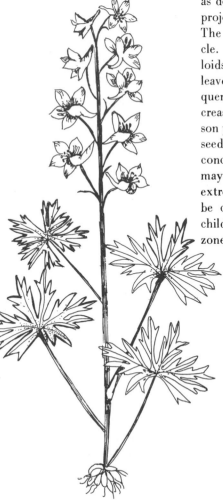

Young plants, seeds

SIGNS OF POISONING

These plants if eaten in quantities cause upset stomach, abdominal cramps, bloating, twitching muscles, nervous symptoms, paralysis, and death.

DUMBCANE, Dieffenbachia , *Dieffenbachia spp.*
(Arum Family)

These evergreen foliage plants are widely grown in greenhouses, homes, restaurants, and lobbies as potted ornamentals. They are planted outdoors in warm southern areas of the United States. The erect perennial herbs, as young plants, have a single green stem. Older plants often develop several stems. All bear near the top a few large oblong leaves without marginal teeth and with sheathing leafstocks. Flowers are tiny; the fruit fleshy. There

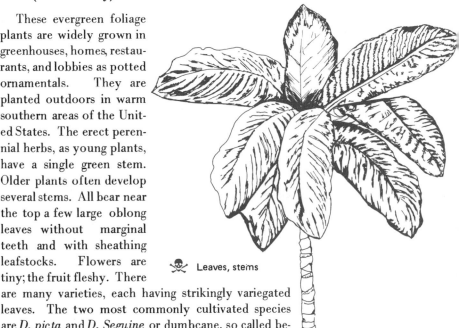

☠ Leaves, stems

are many varieties, each having strikingly variegated leaves. The two most commonly cultivated species are *D. picta* and *D. Seguine* or dumbcane, so called because chewing on it causes temporary speechlessness. *D. picta* has at least two dozen name forms. Its green leaves usually have greenish white dots and patches. *D. Seguine* is a taller, stouter plant with leaves that are slightly heart-shaped at the base, and about twice as long as broad. Colors vary from dark-green to yellowish-green and chartreuse, with variations in white or pale-green. All species contain calcium oxalate needle-like crystals in the stems and leaves. (Native of tropical America)

SIGNS OF POISONING

Biting into, or chewing the stem or leaves soon produces intense burning and irritation of the lips, mouth and tongue. There is severe pain if these areas become swollen. This may cause choking. The swelling can make the tongue motionless, thus interfering with swallowing and breathing. Death may occur if the base of the tongue swells enough to block the air passage of the throat. The skin also may be greatly irritated by the acrid sap.

ENGLISH HOLLY, *Ilex Aquifolium*
(Holly Family)

Berries ☠

The familiar Christmas holly, an evergreen tree up to 40 feet, grows best in the states of Oregon and Washington. The 1½ inch long, dark, lustrous-green leaves growing alternately on each branch are short-stalked, ovalish or oblong, with large triangular-spiny teeth on a wavy margin. The tiny flowers are arranged in small clusters in the leaf axils. The round, red fruit is berry-like with a single seed. American holly *(I. opaca)* is similar in appearance, except that the leaves are dull-green above and yellowish-green beneath. There are many horticultural varieties of this long-cultivated plant, one with silvery-margined leaves and another with yellow-margined, gray-mottled leaves. A number of native holly shrubs and trees are found throughout the United States. *I. vomitoria* or cassena grows from Virginia to Florida and Texas. California holly or toyon is a single, evergreen, native species with thick, leathery, oblongish, sharply-toothed, 2-4 inch long, pointed leaves, and has a cluster of bright-red berries. This shrubby plant is widely planted in California and is often used for Christmas decorations. The berry is the poisonous part on all the species. They are considered especially dangerous to children as they are more apt to eat them in quantities. *(I. Aquifolium* is native of Eurasia and British Isles, others are native of North America)

SIGNS OF POISONING

The berries seem to have no effect upon birds, but in humans, consuming them in large amounts causes nausea, vomiting, diarrhea, and depression of the nervous system. The result may be fatal.

ENGLISH IVY, *Hedera Helix*
(Ginseng Family)

This evergreen, woody, ornamental vine is commonly cultivated throughout the United States for a ground cover, or trained to climb over walls, fences, and trellises. These plants are grown abundantly by nurserymen for display in pots or window boxes. If permitted to use its aerial rootlets to climb, the plant will reach a height of 80-90 feet. The 2-5 inch long leaves are stalked, 3-5 lobed, dark-green above, with paler veins that are yellowish-green beneath and grow alternately on the vine. Leaves are larger, squarish, and without lobes on the flowering branches of mature plants. Stiff branches, toward the top of the vine, bear rounded clusters of small, greenish flowers. The roundish fruit, almost ½ inch in diameter, is a 3-5 seeded black berry. There are many horticultural varieties. Some are white-margined with large or small leaves. Some have leaves that are yellow or variegated with yellow. Most varieties are persistent and hardy, and often escape cultivation. Since ancient times the leaves and berries of ivies have been recognized as poisonous, the foliage more toxic than the berries. On contact, the leaves may irritate the skin. Leaves and berries have been used medicinally. (Native of England to the Caucasus)

SIGNS OF POISONING

The saponin content of the plant may produce severe stomach pains, diarrhea, labored breathing, and eventually coma if the poisonous parts are eaten in quantity. Serious cases have proved fatal.

Leaves, berries

FIG , *Ficus Carica*
(Mulberry Family)

The common fig is a deciduous tree from 15-30 feet tall which is grown in home orchards or for commercial production in California, Florida, and along the Gulf coast of Texas. Elsewhere the tree must receive winter protection and is often retained in tubs. The thick trunk is smooth and gray-barked, but gnarled in very old trees. The 4-9 inch long and nearly as wide leaves are rough, bright-green and 3-5 lobed. Inside the fruit are scores of minute-sized male and female flowers that bloom and mature in the dark interior. The female flowers eventually develop into the *"seeds"*, which are actually small fruits (achenes). The fleshy receptacle or fig comes in many varieties and colors. Some varieties can only develop after pollination. Home garden figs usually bear two crops a year and do not need pollinizing. Each tree regardless of variety has a skin irritant present in its milky sap. The abundant sap is released upon breaking a leaf or picking the fruit, frequently causing dermatitis. (Native of India and Malaya)

Sap in leaves, fruit ☠

SIGNS OF POISONING

The toxic properties in the milky sap may cause symptoms of itching, burning, redness, or blistering on contact. If the raw fruit is eaten unpeeled, these symptoms sometimes appear around the mouth. Adequately ripened fruit has little or no milky sap left.

FLAX , *Linum usitatissimum*
(Flax Family)

Flax has been under cultivation since prehistoric times for its linen fibers and seed oil. Today flax is raised as a farm crop in various areas of the United States, chiefly for the linseed oil obtained from the seeds. This slender annual herb has also escaped from cultivation in many places and is found along roadsides, among other field crops, and in wastelands. The erect and branching plant grows from 1-4 feet high, with mostly alternate leaves which are small, narrow, sharp-pointed, and without marginal teeth. The ½ inch wide delicate blue, or sometimes white flowers, are borne in terminal clusters. Each bloom lasts only a day, but replacements keep coming along. The fruit is a dry capsule, containing ten glossy-brown seeds. The entire plant is poisonous when ingested, especially the immature seeds. These seeds have **caused loss of life due to the tox**-ic concentration of nitrates and the high level of cyanide. **Cooked flax is considered edible.** (Native of Europe)

All parts

SIGNS OF POISONING

Symptoms consist of rapid breathing, which soon changes to gasping, staggering, weakness, then paralysis. Coma and death may follow.

FOUR-O'CLOCK , *Mirabilis Jalapa*
(Four-O'Clock Family)

This is a popular, old-fashioned, showy herb grown in gardens as a perennial in warm-weather climates, and as an annual where winters are cold. It has escaped cultivation in some parts of the southern United States and throughout California. Dwarf and variegated horticultural forms are numerous. The 3-4 foot high plant arises from mounded clumps to form many-branched, erect stems. The 2-6 inch long, opposite leaves (with stalks) are deep-green, smooth, ovalish, and pointed at the tip. The 1 inch across, trumpet-like, red, yellow, white, or striped flowers open in the late-afternoon or earlier in extremely cloudy weather. The fruit is a small, dry, five-ribbed achene, containing many seeds. The thick tuberous roots of the perennials are poisonous if eaten, and the seeds of all forms are poisonous. Dermatitis may result from handling the roots and seeds. (Native of tropical America)

Roots, seeds ☠

SIGNS OF POISONING

Ingesting the poisonous parts of the plant will cause nausea, acute stomach pains, vomiting, abdominal cramps, and diarrhea.

FOXGLOVE , *Digitalis purpurea*
(Figwort Family)

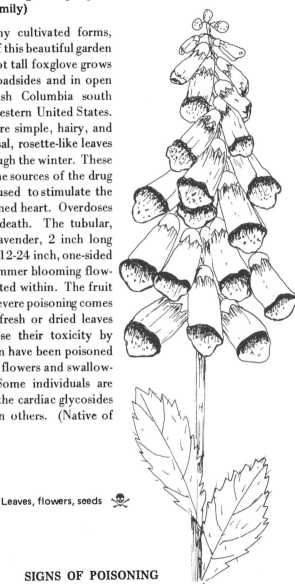

There are many cultivated forms, mostly biennial, of this beautiful garden herb. The 2-5 foot tall foxglove grows naturally along roadsides and in open fields from British Columbia south throughout the western United States. Alternate leaves are simple, hairy, and toothed. The basal, rosette-like leaves remain green through the winter. These leaves are one of the sources of the drug digitalis usually used to stimulate the action of a weakened heart. Overdoses have resulted in death. The tubular, purple or white-lavender, 2 inch long flowers grow in a 12-24 inch, one-sided cluster. These summer blooming flowers are often spotted within. The fruit is a dry capsule. Severe poisoning comes from eating the fresh or dried leaves which do not lose their toxicity by cooking. Children have been poisoned by sucking on the flowers and swallowing the seeds. Some individuals are more sensitive to the cardiac glycosides in the plant than others. (Native of Europe)

Leaves, flowers, seeds ☠

SIGNS OF POISONING

Commonly noticed symptoms are digestive upset, bloody diarrhea, severe headache, mental confusion, blurred vision, trembling, sleepiness, and lack of appetite. Large amounts ingested have caused dangerously irregular heart and pulse beat , convulsions, and death.

GOLDEN CHAIN , *Laburnum anagyroides*
(Pea Family)

This 20-30 foot tall, deciduous tree or large shrub is cultivated in gardens as an ornamental throughout most of the United States. The bark is green. The alternate leaves, composed of three clover-like leaflets, are downy beneath. Golden-yellow, sweet-pea-shaped, about ¾ inch across flowers hang in clusters 4-12 or more inches long. They bloom in the late spring. The fruit is a flat, bean-like pod about 2 inches long that contains eight seeds. Several varieties, some with yellow leaves, are propagated. Golden chain is regarded in England as one of its most poisonous trees. All parts of the plant contain the alkaloid cytisine and other highly poisonous properties, producing an action similar to nicotine. Licorice tasting roots have proved fatal to cattle. The young pods and seeds are highly toxic. Children can be protected from eating these dangerous parts by removing and destroying the flowering portions soon after they have finished blooming. (Native of southern Europe)

All parts ☠

SIGNS OF POISONING

Symptoms consist of nausea, vomiting, diarrhea, headache, nervous excitement, staggering, dilated pupils, convulsions, and coma. Consuming large amounts may be fatal.

HORSECHESTNUT, Buckeye , *Aesculus spp.*
(Buckeye Family)

There are 25 known species belonging to this genus, and a number of highly ornamental varieties have been developed. The most common horsechestnut *(A. Hippocastanum)*, a widely-planted shade and ornamental tree, grows to 100 feet tall. Some of the shrubby species are used as specimen plants, on lawns, or among shrubbery. Buckeyes are native shrubs or trees found on open hillsides in canyons, or in generally streamside-woodland habitats throughout most of the United States. The deciduous leaves of horsechestnuts and buckeyes are opposite, with long stalks. The 5-9 toothed-margined leaflets are arranged finger-fashion. Many clusters, of showy, white, yellow, or red flowers appear with the leaves at the ends of the branches. The large fruit is a spiny capsule, enclosing 1-2 shiny-brown seeds. Leaves, flowers, young sprouts, and seeds hold concentrated amounts of a glycoside aesculin. Roots and branches have a smaller percentage of the poisonous substance. Children have been poisoned from making *"tea"* from the leaves and have died from eating the seeds. Honey made from the California buckeye is also toxic. (Natives of Eurasia and North America)

All parts ☠

SIGNS OF POISONING

Symptoms are vomiting, diarrhea, twitching muscles, weakness, lack of body control, depression or elation, stupor, and dilated pupils. Sometimes paralysis and death result.

HYDRANGEA , *Hydrangea macrophylla*
(Saxifrage Family)

As many as 35 species of these deciduous shrubs or vines with large bold flower clusters and leaves are found growing in the United States. There are numerous cultivated varieties as well as wild species. *H. macrophylla*, widely called hortensia, is the pot or tub hydrangea that florists force for spring bloom. It is also commonly planted as an ornamental shrub which reaches to 12 feet in height. The opposite growing, 3-8 inch long leaves are simple, broadly-oval, pointed at the tip, and coarsely-toothed. These leaves are shiny-green above and lighter-green beneath. The small pink, white, or blue flowers are arranged in dense, globe-shaped, sterile clusters to 1 foot across. Occasionally a form is found with a flat-topped cluster with only the marginal flowers sterile. *H. macrophylla*, is one of several listed by public health authorities as being extremely poisonous. Cyanide compounds are present mostly in the leaves and branches. However, hydrangea buds added to a salad poisoned a family in Florida. (Native of Japan)

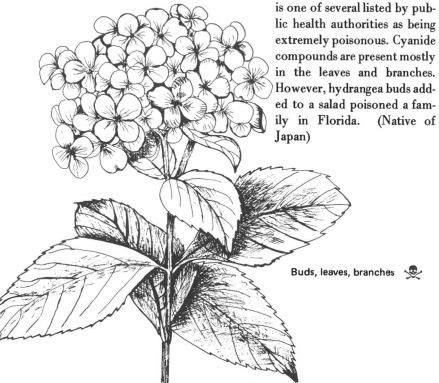

Buds, leaves, branches 💀

SIGNS OF POISONING

Eating the poisonous parts produces severe digestive upset and diarrhea with blood. The heart is affected, causing rapid breathing, gasping, nervous excitement, staggering, convulsions, and has caused death.

IRIS, Flag , *Iris spp.*
(Iris Family)

The familiar garden iris consists of a bearded and beardless group of more than 150 species and they vary greatly in flower color and form. The majority bloom in the spring or early summer. Most of these perennial herbs fall into the bearded group which are raised successfully outdoors in nearly every area of the United States. The leaf is wide and sword-like, while the flower has a beard-like growth along the center line of the claw of the fall (three, outer, downward-bent segments). The rootstock (rhizome) is rather large, plump and smooth, usually growing about half out of the ground with a few small roots beneath. The fruit of all iris is a three-valved, many-seeded pod (capsule). Sweet flag *(Acorus)* grows naturally in moist meadow habitats throughout the north temperate zone. The 2 foot high, stout, grass-like leaves, rise from a thickened, creeping rootstock. The small flowers are greenish; the fruit berry-like. Various other species of wild iris grow in both the eastern and western United States. All iris have an irritant substance in the leaves, but especially in the rootstocks, which produces poisonous effects when eaten in large amounts. The rootstocks sometimes cause a skin rash to develop on contact. Rhizomes of blue flag have been long used medicinally. (Mostly natives of the north temperate zone)

☠ Leaves, rhizomes

SIGNS OF POISONING

Eating the poisonous parts of the plant induces severe digestive upset such as nausea, vomiting, and diarrhea. The severity depends upon the amount ingested and the sensitivity of the individual.

IRISH POTATO, Potato, White Potato
Solanum tuberosum (Nightshade Family)

Potatoes are grown successfully anywhere in the United States by utilizing the coolest season for the early varieties. Since potatoes are not spread by seeds but are propagated by cutting the *"eyes"* from an ordinary potato tuber, few have escaped cultivation. A spreading vine, this herb has compound leaves and leaflets of irregular sizes. White, lavender, or pinkish-lavender flowers are about 1 inch wide. The globe-shaped, ¾ inch wide fruit is yellowish or green, but not often produced in cultivated varieties. Although the wholly ripe tuber is a nourishing and harmless food product, extremely toxic alkaloids of the solanum type are found throughout the plant, particularly in the green parts. Loss of life has occurred from eating the leaves, sprouts, vines, and sun-greened potatoes. Also severe poisoning has resulted from ingesting spoiled potatoes and peelings. It is wise to remove green spots and the sprouts before cooking potatoes as heat does not destroy their poisonous effect. (Native of the high Andes of Old Peru)

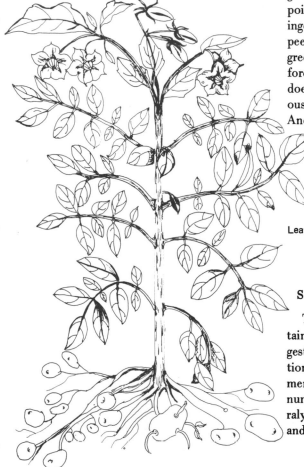

Leaves, sprouts, spoiled parts

SIGNS OF POISONING

The alkaloid poisons contained in the plant cause digestive upset, cold perspiration, lowered temperature, mental confusion, weakness, numbness, dilated pupils, paralysis, circulatory restriction, and death.

JERUSALEM CHERRY , *Solanum Pseudo-capsicum*
(Nightshade Family)

This (usually) annual herb, or evergreen shrub 2-4 feet high, can be grown anywhere in a container for indoor winter decoration and placed outdoors in summer. It is much propagated in greenhouses and sold for use at Christmas time. Jerusalem cherry has many dwarf strains which are more popular than taller kinds because they bear showier fruits. Leaves are deep-green, shiny, wavy, oblongish, and about 4 inches long. The ½ inch wide white flowers are borne in clusters. Globular fruits, about ½ inch in diameter are ordinarily scarlet, but sometimes yellow, and resemble miniature tomatoes. The plant blooms, fruits, and seeds itself throughout the year in the warmer regions of the United States. This entire plant, a relative of the potato, contains dangerous solanum alkaloids. Children have been poisoned by nibbling on the leaves and eating the attractive, bright-colored fruits. (Native of the Old World)

All parts, especially fruit

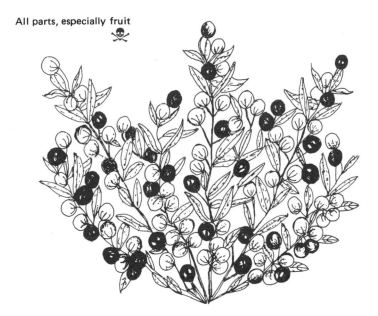

SIGNS OF POISONING

Ingesting parts of the plant may make the mouth unusually moist. There will be changes in the heart rate, profuse perspiration, drowsiness, trembling, extreme weakness, and other circulatory disturbances as well.

LADY'S SLIPPER , *Cypripedium spp.*
(Orchid Family)

These beautiful orchids are found in swamps and wet woodlands, occurring most numerously in the eastern and southeastern states. In the Rockies there are some 40 species. Two native species extend from California northward to British Columbia, and east to Wyoming. Many hybrids have been developed by orchid fanciers who propagate the hardy perennial herbs for greenhouses or outdoor use. There are stemless or stemmed orchids. The flowers that grow on straight stems well above the foliage have a pouch-like lip. An example of this is the common lady's slipper *(C. acaule)* of the eastern United States, which has a pair of oval-shaped, basal leaves 6-8 inches long. This species also has a slender, hairy, scaly stalk that terminates with a green leaflet or bract close to the flower. The three flower petals (sepals) are yellowish-green, slightly-curved and wavy. Beneath the petals is the enlarged lip, usually crimson-pink and veined with a deeper pink. Other species of lady's slipper or moccasin flower, may have blooms in shades of white, yellow, or purplish-brown. All species contain a poisonous substance in the stalks and leaves, which frequently causes dermatitis. (Natives of the northern hemisphere)

☠ Glandular hairs on leaves, stems

SIGNS OF POISONING

As with other plants poisonous by contact, the skin irritation, may be minor and temporary or a painful inflammation with blisters lasting for days or weeks. This depends upon the susceptibility of the person and the severity of the infection.

LANTANA , *Lantana Camara*
(Vervain Family)

This colorful (to 6 feet high) shrub grows naturally in the dry woods of southeastern United States. In moderate climates, lantana is widely cultivated as an outdoor ornamental. Frequently it is grown as a pot plant by florists for its profuse bloom. The dark-green, 2-6 inch long leaves, growing opposite or whorled, are ovalish with toothed margins and roughish above and hairy beneath. These leaves usually are borne on a hairy stem. The small tubular flowers bloom in dense, flat-topped clusters; the stalks being longer than the leafstocks. They show yellow at first, then orange or red, or all three colors may appear in a single cluster. Sometimes the flowers are white or lavender. The fleshy, two-seeded berries, about 1/4-3/8 inches across, turn from greenish to blue-black when ripe. Both foliage and ripe berries contain a toxic substance. Especially dangerous to eat are the green berries for they have a higher concentration of the poison. Hybridizers have developed many varieties of lantana and all species are suspected of causing poisoning. In fact, lantana is rated as one of the main causes of poisoning in Florida. (A native of tropical America, north to Texas and Florida)

All parts, especially green berries

SIGNS OF POISONING

Generally symptoms appear within a day after consuming the poisonous parts. They consist of severe stomach and intestinal upset, weakened muscles, rapid heartbeat, and difficulty in breathing. Kidneys are effected and sensitivity to sunlight is shown. If the vessels carrying blood to the heart collapse, death quickly follows.

LILY-OF-THE-VALLEY , *Convallaria majalis*
(Lily Family)

This is a fragrant spring-blooming perennial herb grown from a horizontal rootstock from which a pip arises (small upright rootstock) which contains a bud and many roots. A single species, it is commonly cultivated in the partial shade of gardens everywhere. Frequently found about abandoned building sites. An identical plant grows wild in the higher Alleghenies from Virginia south to Tennessee and is believed to be a native of that area. The two broad basal leaves are oblong-oval, smooth and shiny. These leaves usually form a dense mat that is persistent and excludes other plants but does not remain evergreen. Slender stalks bear a one-sided row of waxy, bell-shaped, tiny white or pale-pink, nodding flowers. Although seldom seen, the fruit is a red-orange berry about ½ inch in diameter. Leaves, flower, berries, and rootstocks are well-known for their toxicity. They contain dangerous amounts of cardiac glycosides (convallarin and convallamarin). A child lost its life even drinking the water from a vase containing a bouquet of lily-of-the-valley. (Native of Eurasia)

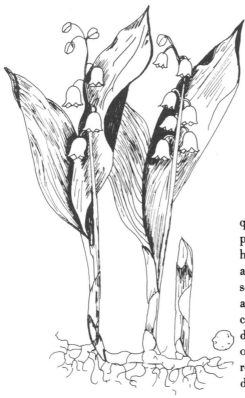

All parts ☠

SIGNS OF POISONING

Eating or chewing small quantities of the poisonous parts produces an irregular heart and pulse beat, usually accompanied by digestive upset. In larger amounts, the active principles cause mental confusion, extreme weakness, depression, and finally collapse of circulation and death. The reaction is much like that of digitalis.

LUPINE , *Lupinus spp.*
(Pea Family)

There are about 100 species of this showy and hardy genus found throughout the United States. Several species are cultivated in gardens, but most lupines grow profusely in fields, on ranges, and mountainsides. California alone has 65 wild species. The plants may be shrubby, from 4-8 feet tall, or herbaceous perennials and annuals, varying in height from 1-4 feet. Alternate leaves are narrow, compound (finger-shaped) and covered with fine hairs on both sides. The pea-like blossoms, in loose clusters to the ends of the branches, may be blue, purple, yellow, pink, or white. The ripe fruits are blackish, flattened, to 3 inch long pods that contain 5-6 kidney-shaped brown seeds. Some, but not all, species of lupine hold toxic alkaloids throughout the entire plant and are a common cause of stock poisoning as a rule. One of the abundant western lupines *(L. caudatus)* is particularly toxic to cattle and horses. The greatest amount of poison is retained in the fully ripened seeds and pods. Eating the seeds in large quantities can be fatal to humans or animals. (Native of Europe and North America)

All parts, especially ripe seeds ☠

SIGNS OF POISONING

Not all poisonous lupines produce the same effects due to the varying amounts of toxic alkaloids found in the different species. Generally, within an hour after consuming the toxic parts, breathing becomes difficult and heavy. The body will begin to twitch; convulsions and unconsciousness may follow. Occasionally death occurs.

MILKWEED , *Asclepias spp.*
(Milkweed Family)

☠ Stems, leaves

Milkweeds are chiefly coarse, erect plants, growing as weeds in dry fields, on hillsides, in woods, and along roadsides. Their profuse milky juice accounts for the name. There are about 60 species of these perennial herbs distributed across the United States. Only a few species are cultivated. Opposite, or whorled leaves are oblong to narrowly egg-shaped (without marginal teeth) and with veins that are rather thick and yellowish. The white, pink, or rose-colored flowers, up to ½ inch in diameter are usually in close, roundish clusters, but sometimes few-flowered clusters sprout at the junction of the leafstock. The large, rough-surfaced, flat seed pods are filled with many seeds, each seed with a tuft of long, silky hairs. Some species of milkweed have medicinal value, but all are noted for their content of resins, and most of them are exceedingly poisonous to humans and livestock. The greatest amount of poison is concentrated in the stout, to 5 feet tall stems and leaves. However, any part of the plant will cause children to have a severe stomach and intestinal upset. **Even harmless species should never be eaten uncooked.** (Native chiefly to North America)

SIGNS OF POISONING

The symptoms appear within a few hours after consuming the leaves and stems. They consist of staggering, labored breathing, high temperature, perspiring, enlarged pupils, muscle spasms and weakness.

MISTLETOE , *Phoradendron spp.*
(Mistletoe Family)

These woody,parasitic,evergreen plants form a bushy growth 1-4 feet in diameter on many kinds of deciduous trees in gardens, along city streets, and in woodlands. Mistletoe is not cultivated but mostly spreads from host to host by birds as they feed. Oak trees are particularly infested. One species *(P. flavescens)* grows on trees from New Jersey and Indiana southward to Florida and Texas. Many other species are distributed throughout the western United States. Opposite, ½-1½ inch long leaves are oblong to obovate, 3-5 veined, leathery, with brittle, olive-green branches. The small flowers are inconspicuous and greenish. The berry-like fruits are pinkish-white and covered by a sticky pulp. These attractive berries are filled with toxic amines. A *"tea"* brewed from the berries has caused fatalities, and both children and adults have died from eating the fresh berries. **Since mistletoe is much used for Christmas decorations, it should be kept out of the reach of young children.** (Natives of North America)

All parts especially berries

SIGNS OF POISONING

Eating the berries will cause acute stomach and intestinal pains, diarrhea, weak pulse, mental disturbances, and the collapse of blood vessels. Death has occurred within 10 hours after ingestion.

MONKSHOOD, Aconite, Wolfsbane *,Aconitum spp.*
(Crowfoot Family)

These showy perennial herbs, to 6 feet high, are found widely as wildflowers in woods, along creeks, and on mountain slopes throughout the United States. *A. columbianum* grows in the high mountains and wet meadows of western Canada and south to California and New Mexico. A European species *(A. Napellus)* is the common ornamental monkshood cultivated in this country. This species is also the source of the powerful drug aconitine, used guardedly as a heart sedative; overdoses are fatal. Basal leaves are divided fingerfashion (3-9 lobed). The flowers are borne mostly in terminal clusters with the upper part of each hood-like. Flower coloring is usually blue or purple, but some species are white or yellow. The fruit is a many-seeded follicle. All species of this genus are dangerously poisonous when taken internally. **The extremely poisonous tuberous root can easily be mistaken for a wild horseradish, sometimes with fatal results.** Children should be warned that the toxic juice found in the flowers, leaves, stems, and black seeds are all poisonous. (Natives of the north temperate zone and Europe)

All parts, especially roots, seeds ☠

SIGNS OF POISONING

Symptoms are burning followed by numbness of the lips and tongue, ringing in the ears, dizziness, severe vomiting, diarrhea, slow and weak heartbeat, muscular weakness, chest pains, convulsions, and death. Ingesting only a small amount of the juice can be fatal within a few hours.

MORNING-GLORY , *Ipomoea purpurea.*
(Morning-Glory Family)

This common, colorful twining vine, is much used in gardens as an ornamental annual. Perennials are not as showy. Alternate, 4-5 inch long leaves are stalked , broadly-oval or heart-shaped, and not lobed. The funnel-shaped flowers generally open in the morning and last only a few hours. *"Heavenly Blue"*, an especially beautiful and popular form, twines from 15-20 feet and its sky-blue flowers are 4-5 inches across. Another form, *"Pearly Gates"*, has large white flowers. The fruit is an egg-shaped or roundish capsule containing many hard seeds. All species of cultivated morning-glory have toxic concentrations of nitrates in their seeds, but those of the two named forms are especially poisonous. Eating 50 or more seeds induces an effect similar to that of marijuana. Wild morning-glory or small bindweed *(Convolvulus arvensis)* commonly found growing in fields and waste places throughout North America, also has poisonous seeds. It has small white or pink-tinged flowers, usually borne in clusters of two. (*C. arvensis* native of Europe, others native of tropical America)

Seeds in quantity

SIGNS OF POISONING

Eating quantities of the seeds causes nausea, digestive upset, hallucinations, blurred vision, mental confusion, lack of coordination, stupor, and coma. The nervous symptoms may show great contrast. Even in the same individual and at the same instance, they can change rapidly.

MOUNTAIN LAUREL , *Kalmia latifolia*
(Heath Family)

This handsome, evergreen, round-topped shrub or small tree is found on rocky slopes and in woodlands from New Brunswick, south to Florida and west to Indiana. It is also used in gardens as an ornamental throughout the United States. Many hybrids have been produced. Alternate or sometimes whorled, 2-4 inch long leaves are glossy and oval, without marginal teeth, with dark-green showing on top and yellowish beneath. Large terminal clusters of flowers, borne on sticky, hairy stems, range in color from rose to white. The fruit is a many-seeded capsule. Both native and cultivated forms are noted for their toxic resins, which are contained in all parts of the plant. The foliage is especially toxic. Delaware Indians used the leathery leaves to make a decoction in order to commit suicide. Children have been poisoned by chewing on *K. latifolia* leaves or sucking juice from the blossoms or by making a *"tea"*. Honey, when made by bees in the area where mountain laurel is grown, has been found to be poisonous. Leaves have been used medicinally. (Native of eastern North America)

All parts ☠

SIGNS OF POISONING

This dangerously poisonous plant generally produces symptoms in about 6 hours. They consist of nausea, intense abdominal pains, vomiting, repeated swallowing, and watering of the eyes, nose, and mouth. In more severe cases breathing becomes difficult; the heartbeat is slower. There is depression, prostration, convulsions, paralysis of the arms and legs, coma, and possible death within 12 to 14 hours.

NARCISSUS, Daffodil, Jonquil , *Narcissus spp.*
(Amaryllis Family)

These welcome spring-flowering perennials are widely grown for ornament either in gardens or indoors in containers. There are many species, varieties and hybrids in cultivation and all bear bulbs which increase from year to year. Basal leaves usually grow the length of the flowering stalk. They are generally narrow and rush-like in the Jonquil, and are strap-shaped and flat in the common daffodil. The prevailing flower colors are white or yellow with many variations. Flowers may be single or in a cluster. The flower of the trumpet narcissus or daffodil has a central, long, tubular crown, but in the jonquil and poet's narcissus the central crown is reduced to a shallow, ring-like cup. The fruit is a three-lobed, many-seeded capsule. Alkaloids are present in all species of narcissus and distributed throughout their plant system. The bulbs contain the greatest amount of alkaloids. Eating only a few bites of a bulb can make a child very ill, while one whole bulb holds enough poison to kill an adult. (Natives of Europe and North Africa)

 All parts, particularly bulbs

SIGNS OF POISONING

Symptoms are nausea, severe stomach and intestinal upset, vomiting, and diarrhea. In addition, there may be trembling, stupor, convulsions, and loss of life.

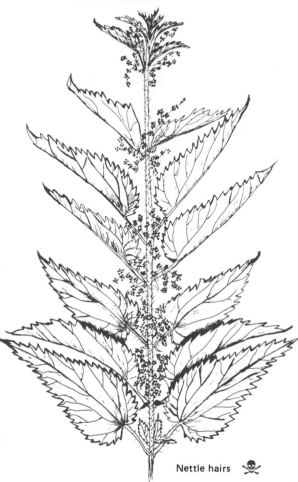

Nettle hairs ☠

NETTLE , *Urtica spp.*
(Nettle Family)

These are unpleasant erect, annual or perennial weedy herbs with stems to six feet tall. They grow in unused areas, ditches, and along streamside woodlands throughout North America. All species can be easily identified by the stinging hairs on their stems and leaves. Opposite (stalked) leaves are usually coarsely toothed. The small, petal-less, greenish flowers sprout from the leaf axils in loose clusters. The fruit is a dry, one-seeded achene. Stiff, sharp hairs on the stems and foliage have a hollow center that extends down from their tips to a bladder-like base which is filled with a caustic chemical fluid (formic acid). Upon con-tact, the hair tips break off and the fluid penetrates the skin. The tip acts like a hypodermic needle. The stinging sensation is extremely painful and has in some instances cause fainting. Nettles are considered among the most painful plants on contact. People who gather nettles to use as a sub-stitute for spinach or *"tea"* usually protect their hands with heavy gloves. Surprisingly enough, some species are capable of producing a good, strong, white linen. (A dwarf species native of Eurasia, others native of North America)

SIGNS OF POISONING

The irritating chemicals in the plant induce itching, burning, and skin inflammation, lasting for different lengths of time. Sometimes this leads to secondary infections, requiring medical attention. Much depends up-on the tenderness of the individual's skin and the percentage of the area contacted.

NIGHTSHADE , *Solanum nigrum*
(Nightshade Family)

Black nightshade or deadly nightshade, an erect, branching, annual herb, is widely distributed in several of its forms throughout the United States. It is an introduced weed that grows from 6 inches to 3 feet high. The plant has become naturalized in waste places, cultivated fields, or around homes. Dull-green, 3-5 inch long (narrow-stalked), leaves are ovalish to lance-shaped, wavy-edged or smooth on the margins, and slightly unequal-sided. The white flowers, each with large yellow anthers, extend from the leaf axils in small drooping clusters. The round fruit, about ¼ inch thick, is dull black when fully ripe. All parts of the plant contain poisonous solanum alkaloids (solanine). Many cases of poisoning have been reported from eating the un-ripened berries. Juice in the wilt-ed leaves is especially toxic and deadly if ingested. Ripe, cooked berries are considered safe to eat as some of the toxicity is destroy-ed in the cooking process. *S. americanum* is a native weed that grows along roadsides and undis-turbed areas everywhere. Its ripe fruit is black (but glossy). Other-wise the plant is essentially the same as *S. nigrum* and equally as poisonous. (Natives of Europe, Tropical and North America)

☠ All parts

SIGNS OF POISONING

A toxic dose produces intense di-gestive disturbances, rapid heartbeat, weak pulse, trembling, dilated eye pu-pils, depression and drowsiness. An overdose brings unconsciousness and death.

OAK , *Quercus spp.*
(Beech Family)

About eighty species of oak are distributed throughout the United States and Canada and are found growing almost anyplace. These woody perennials vary from three foot shrubs to trees up to 150 feet tall. Some are deciduous, whereas the *"live oaks"* retain their leaves during the winter. Alternate leaves are lobed or unlobed, differing much in size and shape; but each species can be recognized by their acorns (seeds) which are borne in a basal cup. The flowers hang in drooping catkins in the spring and their pollen frequently causes an allergy. Oaks have a high content of tannin, particularly in the foliage and acorns. This poisonous substance and bitter taste is alleviated when the acorns are boiled and the water changed several times. Indians removed the outer shell, ground the kernels into meal, and leached the meal many times. Children should be warned against chewing on acorns. Also the leaves and buds have been known to poison livestock, therefore humans should be wary of eating them. Although it takes a large amount of the toxic parts for poisoning, the kidneys are gradually affected. (Natives of the north temperate zone)

Foliage, unleached acorns

SIGNS OF POISONING

Oak poisoning appears after several days or weeks. Symptoms are abdominal pains, constipation, extreme thirst and frequent urination. In severe cases there may be bloody diarrhea, rapid but weak pulse, liver damage, and death. Livestock often die within twenty-four hours after eating quantities of the young foliage and buds.

OLEANDER , *Nerium Oleander*
(Dogbane Family)

Oleander is cultivated as an outdoor ornamental in the southern United States and is particularly widespread in California. This evergreen shrub (to 25 feet tall) has a showy, hardy, long-lasting bloom that is ideally decorative along freeways. It grows as a house plant in the north. Leaves are opposite or in whorls of three tending to be thick and narrow to oblong. These 3-10 inch long (short-stalked) leaves are darker green above, and have a prominent mid-rib beneath. Summer-blooming flowers are borne in clusters and may be white to pink to dark red. They are sometimes double in horticultural forms. The fruit is a cylindrical pod (follicle). All parts of oleander, including the dried leaves, contain deadly glycosides (oleandrin) that stimulate the heart. A child can become dangerously ill from eating a single leaf, or from sucking nectar from the flowers. Also nectar collected by bees produces poisonous honey.

Smoke from burning oleander affects some people. Meat cooked over the branches, and the use of branches as skewers to roast meat over a fire has poisoned the unwary. Dermatitis may result after handling oleander leaves and branches. (Native of Asia)

☠ All parts

SIGNS OF POISONING

The effects produced are similar to those of the drug digitalis. They include digestive upset, bloody diarrhea, dizziness, shallow breathing, fleeting pulse, irregular heartbeat, blurred vision, and drowsiness. Later stages are coma, lung paralysis, and death.

OPIUM POPPY , *Papaver somniferum*
(Poppy Family)

This poppy is an annual herb that grows three to four feet high. Now it is unlawful to grow the *"sleep-bearing"* poppy because of its drug content misuse, although it was once an easily cultivated colorful garden plant in this country and had escaped cultivation in many places. Gray-green basal leaves are coarsely lobed, toothed, and hairy. The stem leaves are clasping and hairy also. Three to four inches across, solitary flowers are white, red, pink or purple. The fruit is a capsule covered with a shield-like cap. Small pores are formed underneath the cap through which the seeds are dispursed. Opium gum comes from the juice of the unripe pod, and the seeds are used for seasoning. This opium is the source of morphine and heroin which has claimed thousands of addicts. All parts of the plant contain heavy concentrations of the alkaloid morphine in the milky juice, especially when the plant is young and green. These plants are poisonous to eat, but it takes high dosages of the less dangerous seeds to poison an individual. All species of poppies contain the same toxic principle to some degree and should be regarded as potentially harmful. (Native of Greece and the Orient)

All parts ☠

SIGNS OF POISONING

Eating the unripe fruit leads to dizziness, delirium, drowsiness, slow breathing, deep sleep, and death. Addiction is not uncommon. Other parts of the plant induce nausea, vomiting, and stomach pains, plus twitching muscles and lack of control of bodily functions.

OSAGE ORANGE , *Maclura pomifera*
(Mulberry Family)

This deciduous tree, the only species of its genus, when leafed out looks like a member of the citrus fruit family. The short trunk was formerly used for bows by the Osage Indians. This trunk is strong and flexible and is covered by a dark, orange-colored bark. The tree, a native from Arkansas to Texas, has become naturalized in other southern and eastern states; elsewhere it is often planted as a windbreak or hedge as the spiny branches produce efficient barriers. Alternate, 1½-4 inches long, pointed leaves are ovate to oblongish, and shining green above. If a male tree is present, the female tree produces greenish flowers in dense clusters. The equally greenish

☠ Milky sap

male flowers are somewhat smaller in size. Female trees bear roundish fruits 2-5 inches across which are much sought after for odd and interesting floral arrangements. These inedible fruits that somewhat resemble bumpy, yellow-green oranges, ripen in autumn, and fall to the ground in short order. It is dangerous for children to swallow the thick pulp of the fruit which can become lodged in the throat and prevent adequate breathing. Also the bark, leaves, and fruit contain a poisonous milky sap (tannin) that has been the cause of dermatitis. (Native of the south-central United States)

SIGNS OF POISONING

Symptoms are mostly due to the inability to release from a person's throat pieces of the tough peelings of the odd fruit. This can cause strangulation leading to death. Irritation of the skin may be the result of contact with the sap.

PEACH , *Prunus Persica, Amygdalus Persica*
(Rose Family)

Hundreds of named varieties of peach trees thrive under a wide range of conditions in orchards and home gardens in most parts of the United States. This deciduous tree is usually under 20 feet tall, with smooth, lance-shaped leaves, from 3-5 inches long. The prevailingly pink blossoms occur singly or doubly. White, red, or striped flowering varieties may have single and double or semi-double blooms and some varieties have purple foliage. The sweet-tasting yellow, red-flushed or white fruit of the familiar peach tree is 2-3 inches across and this fruit surrounds a hard furrowed peach stone. All parts of the tree contain cyanide producing compounds that are released when the peach stone kernels, the bark, and the bitter-tasting leaves are eaten. Adults have been poisoned from eating the kernels; children have died from eating the kernels, chewing on the twigs, and making *"tea"* from the leaves. Also when large amounts of the leaves are ingested, death may result quickly. (Native of China)

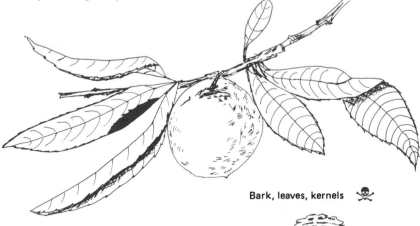

Bark, leaves, kernels ☠

SIGNS OF POISONING

The reaction to the poisoning is rapid, showing little outward signs and causing death in less than an hour if a lethal amount is taken internally. The common symptoms that appear within minutes are gasping, overstimulation, and prostration. Cyanide poisoning produces nervous system involvements as well. Changes in normal breathing and behavior patterns are warnings.

PHILODENDRON , *Philodendron spp.*
(Arum Family)

These evergreen shrubs or vines are among the most popular house plants. They are cultivated in containers for their attractive, deep-green, glossy foliage. There are many horticultural forms, but most in maturity have rather woody stems that eventually grow to unwieldy sizes in need of support. In warm climates some forms grow as strong vines, clinging to tree bark. Some have leaves that are pale-lined above, pale-green but salmon-lined beneath and with red stalks that are both bristly and hairy. The thick, fleshy leaves, variable in size, are usually ovalish or heart-shaped (in some species deeply cut) and pointed at the tip. Sheathing leafstocks are often channeled. Flowers appearing on mature plants, are white, greenish or reddish and resemble mostly minute-sized callas. These flowers are often fragrant; the fruit fleshy. Both leaves and stems are dangerously poisonous when eaten. One leaf can be fatal to a child. Crystals of calcium oxalate in the plants penetrate into the mucus membrane, producing an intense burning sensation and irritation. This irritant substance is very destructive to the kidneys. (Native of tropical America)

 All parts

SIGNS OF POISONING

There is burning of the lips, mouth, and tongue at once after swallowing the poisonous parts of the plant. Painful swelling of the tongue and throat follow, making breathing difficult. Weakness, lack of energy, failure of the kidneys to function, and death are final results.

POISON HEMLOCK , *Conium maculatum*
(Carrot Family)

This evil-smelling but luxuriant weed is found in waste places and gardens from Quebec to Florida, west to California, and throughout the Rocky Mountains. It is a biennial herb that grows from 2-4 feet tall by the second season. Stems are hollow, jointed, much-branched and often purple-spotted. The alternate dark-green leaves have a stem that is similar to a wild carrot minus the hairiness. The toothed leaflets are finely divided and fern-like. Tiny dull-white, slender-branched flowers are in clusters. The small seeds or fruits are ovate and flat, with notched edges. An extract made from the green fruit was formerly used as a sedative by American doctors, but an overdose paralyzes the respiratory organs. Indians used the partly developed seeds to poison their arrows. Ancient Greeks employed this hemlock brewed as a tea to bring about the death of condemned political prisoners, including Socrates. The poisonous principles are coniine and other dangerous alkaloids; the greatest concentration being in the seeds and the hollow, fleshy, white taproot. One mouthful of the root will kill an adult. **Deaths are frequently caused by mistaking the root for parsnip or the seeds for anise. Children have died from sucking and blowing on the stems** and very young children have died from eating the foliage. The plant causes dermatitis on contact as well. (Native of Europe)

SIGNS OF POISONING

🕱 All parts

The action of the poison begins soon after eating any part of the plant. Diarrhea, vomiting, violent stomach pains, trembling, numbness, dilated eye pupils, slow heartbeat, and increasing muscular weakness is followed by paralysis with respiratory failure and then death.

POISON IVY, Poison Oak , *Rhus spp.*
(Sumac Family)

Poison ivy *(R. radicans)* is a woody shrub or vine that climbs high in trees, or along the ground throughout most of the United States. Poison oak *(R. diversiloba)*, a Pacific Coast relative, is an erect shrub, but it does climb some. It grows in low wooded areas, on mountain slopes, or invades gardens and yards in suburbs. In California it is more widespread than any other weed and a colorful addition to the landscape in the fall. Both species have alternate leaves, with three leaflets. Small greenish flowers hang in clusters, and form globe-shaped, yellowish, berry-like fruits.

All parts

Poison ivy leaf margins may be smooth or finely-toothed, or may be variously-lobed, while poison oak leaves are more coarsely-toothed and deeply-lobed. An irritating, non-volatile oil (urushiol) contained in the sap of either species extends to every part, even the pollen. Few people remain immune after the oil comes in contact with the skin. To make matters worse wind and smoke carry the oil through the air. Animals, articles of clothing, or objects which have touched the plants can transmit the poison also. Internal poisoning has occurred after eating the berries or leaves, causing serious digestive upset and injury to the alimentary canal membrane. (Natives of North America)

SIGNS OF POISONING

Symptoms, upon contact, may amount to a burning, itching rash to broken blisters that spread rapidly when scratched. In severe cases the infection covers the entire body, producing swelling and fever. Sometimes hospitalization is required, and has occasionally proved fatal. Kidney damage has been noted where deaths occurred.

POKEWEED, Poke, Inkberry , *Phytolacca americana*
(Pokeweed Family)

This handsome weed, a strong-smelling shrub-like perennial herb to 10 feet tall, is commonly found in open fields, wastelands, roadsides, disturbed areas especially in wet places of the eastern United States. It is also a quick growing weed in similar places on the west coast. Stout stems are purple or green. Alternate, 6-9 inch long, often red-veined leaves, are oblong-oval with base and tip pointed, without marginal teeth. White flowers hang in drooping clusters. The round fruit, to ½ inch in diameter, is a ten-seeded, juicy, shiny, purple-black berry, often used in pies. Berries and roots are a source of a drug used in medicine, but the plant contains deadly poisonous alkaloids, (saponins) chiefly in the long, fleshy taproot, resembling a horseradish. Consuming the roots has produced fatal results. Eating of more than ten raw berries has been known to cause adults to be seriously poisoned, and a small child can be fatally poisoned by eating two or three uncooked berries. The seeds are almost as poisonous as the roots. Young shoots, resembling asparagus, are edible if thoroughly boiled in two changes of water. Otherwise they are known to be dangerously toxic. (Native of eastern North America)

☠
All parts, especially root

SIGNS OF POISONING

Consuming raw pokeweed first produces a burning sensation in the mouth. About 2 hours later nausea, vomiting, severe cramps, and watery diarrhea are evident. Other symptoms are weakness, blurred vision, difficulty in breathing, perspiring, spasms, and convulsions. The poisoning may be fatal if recovery does not take place within 24 hours.

PRIVET, Prim , *Ligustrum vulgare*
(Olive Family)

This deciduous hedge or shrub plant to 15 feet high is one of the most widely grown privets in gardens throughout the United States. It has become naturalized in woods and along creeks everywhere. Opposite, 1¾-2½ inch long leaves are oblong-oval and without marginal teeth. The leaf coloring is dark-green above and light-green beneath. Small white flowers are borne in terminal clusters not over 2 inches long, these ripen into drooping clusters of small black or bluish 1-4 seeded, wax-coated, berry-like fruits. There are many horticultural forms with golden, variegated, white-margined, or otherwise marked foliage. One variety has yellow fruit. A poisonous factor (andromedotoxin) is in the foliage and berries, the foliage containing more poison than the berries. Most reported cases of human poisoning have occurred from eating the ripe berries, sometimes causing fatal poisoning to children. Other species of privet are equally as dangerous. Small children can be protected from the attractive berries in home gardens by keeping the flower-bearing branches trimmed off. (Native of Europe and northern Africa)

Berries, leaves

SIGNS OF POISONING

Poisoning by privet consists of severe digestive disturbances such as pain, vomiting, and diarrhea. Kidney damage and fall of blood pressure occur also. Intaking a lethal dose can cause death within a few hours.

RHODODENDRON, Azalea , *Rhododendron spp.*

All parts ☠ (Heath Family)

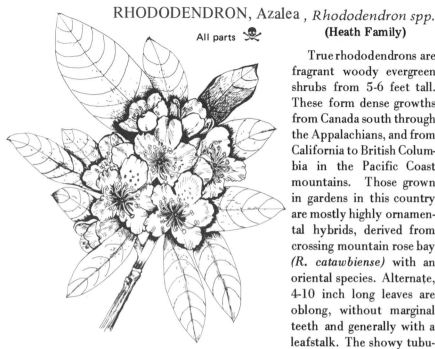

True rhododendrons are fragrant woody evergreen shrubs from 5-6 feet tall. These form dense growths from Canada south through the Appalachians, and from California to British Columbia in the Pacific Coast mountains. Those grown in gardens in this country are mostly highly ornamental hybrids, derived from crossing mountain rose bay *(R. catawbiense)* with an oriental species. Alternate, 4-10 inch long leaves are oblong, without marginal teeth and generally with a leafstalk. The showy tubular or funnel-shaped flowers bloom in crowded heads, and may be white or lilac-purple, varying to rose-purple. The fruit is a dry capsule. The mature azaleas are native, chiefly deciduous shrubs. Many varieties are cultivated in gardens. Alternate leaves are oblongish, and have a stalk. Funnel-shaped flowers are usually in terminal, umbel-like clusters, varying from white through every hue of pink to deep crimson, or else striped. The fruit is a dry pod filled with numerous small seeds. All parts of these plants contain dangerously toxic resins (andromedotoxins) but especially the foliage. Eating two leaves can cause serious illness. Sucking the flowers is also dangerous. The poison has shown up in honey made by bees known to have visited the blossoms. (Natives of North America and Asia)

SIGNS OF POISONING

The time varies in the appearance of symptoms, depending largely upon the amount consumed. Among animals the average is 6 hours. Evident is acute digestive upset, salivation, nasal discharge and increased tear formation. In severe cases paralysis, stupor, and depression of the heart and the central nervous system occurs. Some deaths have been reported.

RHUBARB , *Rheum Rhaponticum*
(Buckwheat Family)

A stout, deep-rooted, perennial herb, rhubarb is frequently grown in home vegetable gardens or flower beds for its pleasantly acid leafstalks which are used principally in the spring for sauces and pies. Basal, long-stalked leaves are 12-30 inches long and divided or veined, finger-fashion. The green or red leafstocks are channeled or sheathed. These leafstalks are roundish, about 1 inch wide and often wavy-margined. The small, greenish-white flowers at the end of a central stalk are borne in numerous, dense, panicled clusters. The fruit is a strongly-winged achene. Rhubarb is considered the most dangerous of all plants in a garden because of the lethal amounts of oxalic acids concentrated in the leaf blades. This leafy part is as poisonous as uncooked pokeweed, and cooking does not reduce the toxicity. Eating only a small amount of a blade has caused painful poisoning. Death has also occurred from eating fried blades. The oxalic acids crystalize in the kidneys, damaging them severely. Contact with the leaves sometimes causes skin irritation. (Native of Siberia)

☠ Leaves

SIGNS OF POISONING

Ingestion of large amounts of raw or cooked leaf blades can cause severe abdominal pains and cramps, nausea, vomiting, weakness, labored breathing, internal bleeding, reduced urine formation, convulsions and coma followed rapidly by death.

ROSARY PEA, Precatory Bean, Indian Licorice
Abrus precatorius, **(Pea Family)**

This plant of many names is a woody perennial vine to 20 feet in length. It grows as a weed trailing on the ground in citrus groves or twining on fences in Florida. Sometimes it is propagated in warm greenhouses on lattice. Generally the seeds are brought into the United States by tourists who have visited tropical areas; the seeds having been prepared, as rosaries, necklaces, bracelets, and toys. Alternate leaves are compound, with 10-15 pairs of small oblong leaflets, about ½ inch long, which fold up in cloudy weather. The small pea-like stalked flowers form a loose cluster, arising in the leaf axil. Colors may be pink, red, or purple, rarely white. The fruit is a many-seeded pod to 1½ inches long, which is covered with fine hairs. These seeds are oviform, 1/4-3/8 inches long, glossy bright scarlet or orange with a black marking at one end. The seeds hold abrin, one of the most deadliest poisons known. It takes less than one well-chewed seed to kill an adult. Swallowing unchewed seeds is less dangerous due to the hard covering, usually passing undigested. People have even been poisoned by stringing the seeds with a pierced finger. (Native of India)

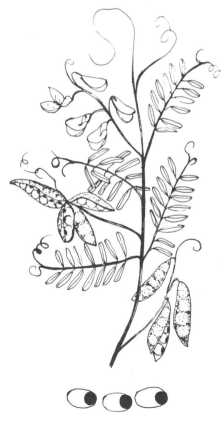

Bean ☠

SIGNS OF POISONING

Symptoms appear in 1-3 days. They consist of nausea, vomiting, acute abdominal and muscular cramps, diarrhea, weakness, cold sweat, drowsiness, weak but fast pulse, trembling, coma, circulatory-respiratory failure, and death. Abrin is known to cause the blood cells to clump and break down. It injures other cells as well.

SNEEZEWEED , *Helenium spp.*
(Sunflower Family)

Sneezeweeds are rather coarse annual or perennial herbs found commonly in low wet meadows, along stream banks, or on mountain slopes below 10,000 foot elevations throughout North America. A few species, all perennials, are cultivated in gardens and grow to 6 feet tall depending upon the variety. The odor of the late summer or fall blooming flowers is said to induce sneezing. The alternate, nearly smooth leaves are usually lance-shaped but some are as thin as grass. The stiff stems may be branched or unbranched near the top. Daisy-like ray flowers in shades of yellow, orange, red or copper, surround the center cone-shaped or flat-topped disk flowers of brownish tones. In the perennials, the plants are reproduced by offshoots from the thick rootstocks. The poisonous substance (dugaldin), sim-

All parts

ilar in action to aconitine of monkshood, is present in all species of sneezeweed, and extends to all parts of the plant. *Helenium spp.* also retain their poison when dry. Using a large amount of seeds from a wild species in baked bread proved to be poisonous. Sneezeweeds are among the most dangerous plants in this country to range stock and are unsafe for human consumption. (Natives of North America)

SIGNS OF POISONING

Sneezeweed poisoning causes vomiting, weakness, trembling, rapid and irregular heart and pulse beat, labored breathing, spasms, convulsions, and fatality. Liver and kidney damage was noted in post mortem examinations of livestock.

SNOW-ON-THE-MOUNTAIN , *Euphorbia marginata*
(Spurge Family)

This popular annual herb to 2 feet tall, is widely planted as an ornamental in gardens. It is native to the prairie soils of South Dakota to Texas. The bushy much-branched plant has also escaped cultivation in the eastern states. Smooth-margined, stalkless leaves are oblongish, and 1-3 inches long. The lower part of the leaves are green with the upper portion white-margined. Bracts of the flower cluster, for which the plant is grown, are white and showy while the true flowers are insignificant and have no petals or sepals. The fruit is a roundish, three-lobed capsule. Both native and cultivated forms contain toxic acid substances (euphorbon) in their milky sap. Upon contact with the skin, the juice may cause severe blistering, and intense pain if rubbed in open cuts or in the eyes. Eating parts of the plant produces harmful irritations in the

mouth, throat and stomach. Bees visiting the flowers yield poisonous honey. All members of the Spurge family are notorious for their possession of toxic properties, resident in their milky juices. They are dangerous if taken internally. (Native of the Great Plains of the United States)

Milky sap, all parts ☠

SIGNS OF POISONING

Snow-on-the-mountain is one of the most frequent causes of dermatitis. Contact with the poisonous sap in the leaves or flowers may cause a painful, itching skin eruption which can become serious. Consuming parts of the plant is hazardous, and in rare cases has proved fatal.

SOUR DOCK, Sorrel , *Rumex Acetosa*
(Buckwheat Family)

This is a stout perennial herb to 3 feet tall, long used as a potherb among Europeans. The rigid stemmed plant has become naturalized in North America and is found growing in gardens, pastures, meadows, and wastelands. Many consider it a troublesome weed. The basal to 5 inch long leaves are thin, ovalish and arrow-shaped at the base. The color is light-green. Stem leaves tend to narrow to a sharp point. The flowers are of two kinds, stamens only, or pistils only, found on separate plants. These green flowers in branching spikes are inconspicuous, but later the brown-red seeds are very noticeable. Quite often the entire plant turns brown-red in dry sterile fields. The fruit is an achene with a papery, three-sided covering. Indians ground the ripe seeds into a meal to make mush. Tender sour-tasting young leaves are used in mixed salads, or cooked as *"greens"*; they contain large amounts of potassium oxalate. Eating quantities of raw leaves has resulted in human poisoning and loss of livestock. Leaves if cooked after one change of water are considered safe. This has been reported about several other species of *Rumex*, each have varying amounts of poisonous oxalates. Dermatitis may occur by contact with the plant. (Native of Europe and Asia)

☠ Leaves in quantity

SIGNS OF POISONING

Oxalate poisoning may appear within 2-6 hours after ingesting large amounts of the leaves. Symptoms are loss of appetite, listlessness, labored breathing, loss of muscle control, depression, coma, and occasionally death within 10 hours.

THORNAPPLE, Jimsonweed , *Datura Stramonium*
(Nightshade Family)

This imported weed is a showy annual herb 5 feet high. It has become naturalized in open areas of the foothills, dry pastures, and vacant city lots over most of the country. The plant has a thick, many-branched central stock. Alternate, 5-6 inch long leaves are smooth, broad and coarsely-toothed. The erect five-pointed, trumpet-like flowers, about 4 inches long, are white or pale-violet. Egg-shaped fruits are about 2 inches long, and covered with stout spines, the longest at the tip of the capsule. The fetid plant's strong odor is said to cause drowsiness. Both seeds and leaves yield narcotic drugs used in medicine. Powerful alkaloids (hyoscyamine) in the plant make the juice poisonous, deadly so when wilted. In the recent past, a man in California died from imbibing the juice and children have died from swallowing the seeds. Even sucking nectar from the flowers has poisoned children. Eating boiled plants produces irrational behavior. Early California Indians knew this and gave their children potions made from the plant to obtain visions especially upon reaching puberty, but expert shamans regulated the dosage. All parts of the plant result in poisoning if eaten and large amounts are fatal if not quickly treated by a physician. Contact with the leaves and flowers will cause dermatitis. (Native of Asia)

☠ All parts

SIGNS OF POISONING

Symptoms are abnormal thirst, distorted sight, weakness, dizziness, staggering, irrational behavior, delirium, incoherence, dilated eye pupils, and coma. Convulsions and circulatory collapse may preceed death.

TOBACCO , *Nicotiana spp.*
(Nightshade Family)

There are many species of this genus of annual or perennial herbs or shrubs. Several are cultivated in gardens as *"flowering tobacco"* or *"Nicotiana".* *N. Tabacum* is the agricultural product, but it is also used as a garden plant. Wild tobaccos are widely distributed throughout the areas. Tobacco grows from 2-20 feet tall and has mostly large soft leaves. Entire plants are more or less covered with short sticky hairs. Alternate leaves are smooth-margined and simple. Sweet-scented, tubular flowers forming clusters at the ends of the branches are white, green-

ish-yellow or purple. The flowers generally open in the evening, but remain open on sunless days also. The fruit is a 2-4 celled dry capsule, containing many tiny seeds. All species of tobacco have a high content of the poisonous alkaloid nicotine, especially in the foliage. Deaths have occurred when the leaves were used in a salad. A wild species known to have been cooked as *"greens"* severely poisoned a family, with one member dying. Sucking on the flowers has been known to poison children. The toxic juice is quickly absorbed in the body where it comes in contact with open cuts or sores. Smoking the dried and cured leaves is considered a dangerous practice by most physicians, including the Surgeon General. (Natives of tropical America)

SIGNS OF POISONING

The effects in all species are largely nervous. They consist of shivering, shaking, twitching muscles, rapid heartbeat, staggering, weakness, staring, blindness, and death. Other symptoms are nausea, vomiting, diarrhea, and abdominal pains.

All parts ☠

TOMATO, *Lycopersicum esculentum*
(Nightshade Family)

The annual garden tomato belongs to a group of from 10-12 species, all of which are closely related to the deadly nightshade. This herb is spreading, hairy, and strong-smelling, growing from 3-6 feet high. Alternate leaves are compound, often with smaller leaflets interspersed with larger ones. The small yellow, usually nodding, flowers are shallowly bell-shaped. The pulpy red or yellow fruit is 2-3 inches in diameter (much larger in some cultivated forms), the sides more or less grooved. This species is rarely cultivated, but thousands of varieties have been derived from it. For centuries the fruit was thought to be poisonous and planted in gardens as an ornamental. Although we now know fresh tomatoes are harmless, the foliage and vines do contain alkaloid poisons (solanine). Children have been severely poisoned from making a *"tea"* from the leaves, and livestock have died from eating the foliage and vines. (Native of South America)

Leaves, stems ☠

SIGNS OF POISONING

Digestive upsets consist of nausea, vomiting, abdominal pains, constipation or bloody diarrhea. Nervous effects are sluggishness, abnormal flow of saliva, labored breathing, trembling, weakness, loss of feeling, and paralysis. Eating quantities of the poisonous parts can be fatal.

WHITE SNAKEROOT, Richweed , *Eupatorium rugosum or E. urticaefolium*
(Sunflower Family)

This branching perennial herb from 2-4 feet tall grows as a devastating weed in rich woodlands, shaded pastures, fields, and along roadsides from Canada south to Georgia, west to Minnesota, and south to Texas. The plant tends to grow abundantly after the removal of timber for a year or two, but is not persistent in gardens unless deliberately cultivated. The opposite, long-stalked leaves are smooth, thin, sharply-toothed and ovalish, but broad toward the base. They are 3-5 inches long. Showy snow-white blooms, in a loosely branched terminal cluster, bear fruit (achene) with a downy white crown like ageratum. The toxic principle is tremetol, which is present throughout the entire plant. Cows eating the plant develop a disease called trembles and transmit it to humans in a disease long known as *"milk-sickness"*. This disease affects dairy products and the meat of the poisoned animals. Milk-sickness was the most frequent cause of death among early day settlers who were unaware of the toxicity of the plant. It is believed one of the victims was Abraham Lincoln's mother. Today the chief danger lies in using raw milk from a family cow in places where white snakeroot grows. (Native of eastern North America)

☠ All parts

SIGNS OF POISONING

Symptoms of milk-sickness are nausea, extreme thirst, repeated vomiting, abdominal pains, loss of appetite, weakness, trembling, jaundice from liver damage, constipation, labored breathing, delirium, and coma. If not fatal, recovery is gradual.

YELLOW JESSAMINE, Carolina Jessamine
Gelsemium sempervirens
(Logania Family)

All parts

A beautiful woody evergreen vine from 10-20 feet tall, jessamine is commonly found trailing in woods and fields, or climbing on trees and fences from Virginia to Texas. The gray-stemmed vine is also used extensively to cover porches and trellises, or as a greenhouse plant, almost everywhere. Mostly opposite, short-stalked, 2½-4 inch long leaves are oblongish, smooth-margined, and shiny. The bright yellow, fragrant tubular flowers are about 1 inch long and usually clustered around the leaf axil. The fruit is a flattened, short-beaked, about ¾ inch long pod with a winged seed. The entire plant contains a number of alkaloids (gelsemine) related to strychnine. It is classed as one of the ten most poisonous plants in North Carolina. The greatest amount of poison is in the rootstock and the flower nectar. This rootstock is the source of a strong sedative drug, and overdoses are not uncommon. Children have died from sucking the nectar from the blossoms. The nectar has also poisoned bees, and honey made from the nectar is toxic. Ingesting the leaves has been fatal to livestock. Flowers, leaves, and roots cause dermatitis. (Native of the southeastern United States)

SIGNS OF POISONING

Symptoms are heavy perspiring, intense abdominal cramps, muscular weakness, shallow breathing, convulsions, paralysis, and death due to respiratory failure unless quick action is taken.

YEW, Ground Hemlock , *Taxus spp.*
(Yew Family)

These distinctive non-fragrant evergreen shrubs or trees to 75 feet tall, have dark, dense foliage and thin, flaking, scaled bark. Two cultivated species *(T. baccata* and *T. cuspidata)* are imports and widely used around homes as ornamentals. Western Yew *(T. brevifolia)* grows as a tree in forests and ravines from California to Montana, British Columbia and Alaska. Ground hemlock *(T. canadensis)* a shrub about 5 feet tall, is native to deep woods from Kentucky to the north-central and northeastern states to Canada.

☠ Foliage, seeds, bark

Alternate ½-1 inch long leaves are rigid and very narrow, the lower part yellowish, with a prominent midrib. Male and female flowers on different plants, are without sepals or petals. Only the female flowers produce the fleshy, scarlet, cup-shaped fruit which has one stony seed. All species contain toxic alkaloids (taxine) in their juice, particularly in the foliage, bark, and seeds. Ingesting these parts is extremely dangerous, whether fresh or dried. The seeds are deadly if chewed. Consuming large amounts of the foliage and bark can be fatal. (Natives of Europe, Japan, and North America)

SIGNS OF POISONING

Death is usually sudden and without warning if the degree of poisoning is great. Swallowing smaller amounts induces vomiting, nausea, diarrhea, abdominal cramps, trembling, breathing difficulties, and dilated pupils.

ZEPHRANTHES, Atamasco Lily
Zephyranthes Atamasco, (Amaryllis Family)

A spring-flowering bulbous perennial herb, this species usually forms clumps in damp wooded areas or fields from Pennsylvania to Florida, and throughout the Gulf States. In the wild, the flowers appear a few days after a rain, thus they are often called rain lilies. The bulbs of this fairy lily are also cultivated in home gardens or used as potted house ornamentals. The thick clumps, appearing in the fall or early spring are bluish-green. Narrow, rather grass-like, flat, basal leaves are 4-10 inches long. An erect solitary flower is borne at the top of a leafless, hollow stem, about 12 inches long. White, or white tinged with purple, flower-cups are funnel-shaped and divided into six lobes. The fruit is a three-celled capsule. The size of the onion-like, brown-coated, white-fleshed bulb is about 1 inch in diameter. Both leaves and bulbs contain poisonous alkaloids, the bulb having the largest concentration. Cases of poisoning have occurred in livestock, especially in the spring when the bulb is easily pulled out of the moist ground, and the leaves tempt hungry animals. A disease known as *"staggers"*, common to horses of the southeastern states, is said to be caused by this herb. Eating large amounts has proved fatal. (Native of the eastern United States)

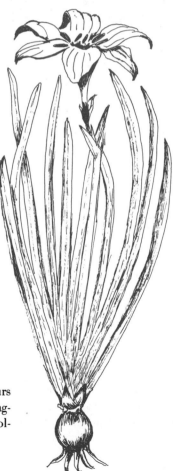

☠ Leaves, bulbs

SIGNS OF POISONING

Within a period of less than 48 hours the symptoms appear, producing staggering, vomiting, bloody diarrhea, collapse, and sometimes death.

Notes on other dangerous plants that can cause illness or death when taken internally, or else may be poisonous on contact. This list is far from complete and new plants found to contain toxic compounds are constantly being added. The four families with the largest number of species known to be troublesome are classified in order as: Pea (about 102 species), Crowfoot, Sunflower, and Spurge.

AKEE, *Blighia sapida.* This small, stiff-branched tree of the Soapberry family is cultivated in frost-free parts of California and southern Florida. The leathery leaves are compound. Leaflets, 4-6 inches long are arranged three, four, or five-paired, feather-fashion. The over or under-ripe fruit, fruit wall, and large, round black seeds are poisonous when eaten. Only the white portion of the mature fruit is edible.

APRICOT, *Prunus Armeniaca.* Rose family. The kernels inside the fruit seeds contain cyanide. Eating them in large quantities has caused death. (Not illus.)

BANEBERRY, *Actaea spp.* Several species of this perennial herb of the Crowfoot family are scattered throughout the United States. They grow to 3 feet tall in rich woods. The leaves are large, spreading, twice or thrice compound with sharply-toothed margins. All parts of the plant are poisonous, but especially the thick rhizome and the red or white berries.

BIRD OF PARADISE, *Poinciana Gilliesii.* A tropical shrub or small tree of the Pea family, cultivated outdoors in the warm regions of the United States and confined as a large potted plant elsewhere. Alternate leaves are twice compound, with very numerous ½-¾ inch long leaflets arranged in pairs, feather-fashion. Children eating the poisonous green ¾ inch long and about ¾ inch wide seed pods, have become seriously ill.

BLOODROOT, *Sanguinaria canadensis.* This wildflower belongs to the Poppy family, and is common in rich woodlands from southern Canada to Florida and Texas. The red perennial root sends up a single 4-6 inch wide, lobed leaf in early spring. A beautiful white flower with 8-12 petals appears before the leaf unrolls. The entire plant is poisonous. Contact with the red sap may cause dermatitis.

BRACKEN FERN, *Pteridium aquilinum.* Several varieties of bracken belonging to the Fern family are distributed throughout the United States. Ingesting the old green or dry fronds in quantities has resulted in poisoning. (Not illus.)

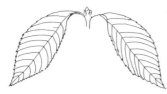

BURNING BUSH, WAHOO, *Euonymus atropurpureus.* A deciduous shrub or small tree of the Staff-tree family which grows 8-20 feet high. This plant is native to the eastern United States but is cultivated in gardens everywhere. The 2-5 inch long, opposite leaves are simple, ovalish, finely-toothed, and hairy beneath. The leaves, the four-lobed scarlet fruit, and the bark have been found poisonous to children when chewed upon. In olden times the bark was used medicinally.

BUTTONBUSH, *Cephalanthus occidentalis.* This is the cultivated 5-15 foot high shrub belonging to the Madder family. Other species grow naturally in swamps throughout the United States. The 3-5 inch long leaves without marginal teeth are opposite or whorled. The poisonous part is in the bitter-tasting juice of the leaves. The bark has been used in medicine.

CANARY BIRD BUSH, *Crotalaria agatiflora.* This is an evergreen shrub of the Pea family, cultivated in warmer areas of California and Florida for its unique flowers which bloom strung along the flower spike (to 14 inches long) like yellow-green birds. Alternate leaves are gray-green and divided into three, inch long leaflets. The loose seeds inside the roundish pod are poisonous. The plant is valued for green manuring in the south.

CASHEW, *Anacardium occidentale.* This is a tropical evergreen tree of the Sumac family, cultivated in warm regions of the United States to produce the cashew-nut. The simple, rather leathery alternate leaves are 4-9 inches long and 2-3½ inches wide. Kernels from the shells are edible when roasted, but the kidney-shaped shells contain a poisonous oil which causes skin irritation similar to poison ivy or oak. Smoke from burning shells causes skin irritation.

CHERRY LAUREL, *Prunus Laurocerasus*. Not a true laurel, this evergreen shrub or small tree of the Rose family is a popular garden plant in warmer sections of the United States. It is often used as a hedge. Short-stalked, 2½-6 inch leaves are oblongish, remotely or not at all toothed, and shiny. All parts of the plant release cyanide. Particularly poisonous are the leaves, bark, and the seeds inside the dark purple fruit. Amygdalin is one of the cyanogenetic glycosides found in *Prunus spp.*, known to cause lethal levels of hydrocyanic acid (prussic acid) build up in the blood.

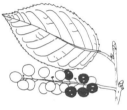

CHOKE CHERRY, *Prunus virginiana*. This shrub or small tree belonging to the Rose family, is distributed naturally throughout eastern North America. There are two western species (*demissa* and *melanocarpa*) that are closely related. The alternate leaves are simple, thin, egg-shaped, and sharply-toothed. Juice from the wilted leaves can be dangerously poisonous. Eating a large quantity of the red or red-purple berries without removing the pits which contain cyanide has caused the death of children. Chokecherries make excellent syrup and jelly. Cooking frees the volatile cyanide.

CLIMBING LILY, GLORY LILY, *Gloriosa superba*. This is a slender, weak-stemmed, tuberous-rooted vine of the Lily family, generally grown as a potted plant, but is cultivated outdoors in the southern part of the United States. The alternate 4-7 inch long and ½-1 inch wide leaves are simple, and lance-shaped. The tips of the leaves extend into tendrils for climbing. Outdoors the 2-3 inch long yellow flowers bloom in the fall. All parts are extremely poisonous, especially the tubers.

COMMON BOXWOOD, BOX, *Buxus sempervirens*. This ornamental evergreen of the Boxwood family is widely used as a hedge, individual shrub, or as small trees. ½-¾ inch long, opposite leaves are simple, ovalish, leathery, dark glossy-green on the upper surface and lighter-green or whitish beneath. The leaves and twigs have caused serious illness when eaten in large amounts. Leaves were used medicinally in the past and thought to be a good cathartic. Clippings have caused stock mortality.

CORN COCKLE, *Agrostemma Githago.* This weed is a tall, silky, grayish winter annual of the Pink family. It grows among wheat, other cultivated crops, and along roadsides throughout the United States. A few varieties are grown as ornamentals. 2-4 inch long, opposite leaves are narrow with parallel edges. Stems and leaves are covered with white hairs. The many black seeds, each covered with a pitted surface, are the source of poisoning. *(Lychnis Coeli-rosa* or *Silene)*

COW PARSNIP, MASTERWORT, *Heracleum lanatum.* This coarse herb of the Carrot family grows to 8 feet high and nearly as wide in moist places throughout North America. Cattle have been reported poisoned by the plant—however, if plenty of good grazing is provided it seems to cause no trouble. Dermatitis is probable to humans. (Not illus.)

CRINUM LILY, SWAMP LILY, *Crinum americanum.* This is not a true lily, but a lily-like herb of the Amaryllis family with a large, thick, bulbous root. It is widely grown in warm areas for its attractive clusters of white flowers. The few leaves are thick, long and narrow. An 18-24 inch stalk usually appears before the leaves. The bulb is considered the most dangerous part of the plant, causing intestinal upset if ingested.

CURSED CROWFOOT, *Ranunculus sceleratus.* A member of the Crowfoot family commonly found in marshy places in the northern United States, its main difference to a regular buttercup is flowers which have enlarged downy receptacles surrounded by very thin petals. Long-stalked basal leaves are nearly round with wavy margins. Alternate stem leaves are palmately veined and lobed. The high content of toxic substances (anemenol) make the entire plant dangerous.

CYCLAMEN, *Cyclamen persicum* or *C. indicum.* There are about 20 species of this perennial herb belonging to the Primrose family. *C. persicum* is the common potted cyclamen sold by florists and is also grown outdoors. Long-stalked, 2½-3 inch wide leaves are all basal, roundish, heart-shaped, and have margins with rounded teeth. The outstanding white, or dark-rose, 2 inch wide flowers resemble shooting stars. Tubers are the poisonous part of the plant.

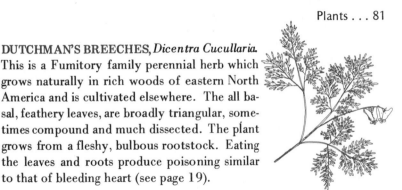

DUTCHMAN'S BREECHES, *Dicentra Cucullaria.*
This is a Fumitory family perennial herb which
grows naturally in rich woods of eastern North
America and is cultivated elsewhere. The all basal, feathery leaves, are broadly triangular, sometimes compound and much dissected. The plant
grows from a fleshy, bulbous rootstock. Eating
the leaves and roots produce poisoning similar
to that of bleeding heart (see page 19).

ELDERBERRY, ELDER, *Sambucus canadensis.*
A Honeysuckle family shrub which grows 6-12 feet
high in woods, waste places and along streams from
Canada south to Florida and Arizona. Other species,
are common shrubs from the Rockies to the Pacific
coast. Opposite leaves are compound, with toothed margins. Short-stalked, 2½-6 inch long leaflets
taper at the tip and are mostly seven in number. Roots, stems and leaves
of all species are dangerously poisonous. Uncooked berries may cause
vomiting and diarrhea. Children making whistles or blowguns out of
dried stems have been poisoned. The black berries are used for jelly and
wine.

ELEPHANT-EAR, *Colocasia antiquorum.* A
tuberous rooted herb of the Arum family, this
bedding plant 6-9 feet high and as wide is grown
in warm areas of the United States for its foliage.
Many prevailing colors. The green variations
have leaves about 2 feet long; leafstocks 4-5 feet
long. The major danger lies in the sharp calcium
oxalate crystals present in the plant. Upon
chewing any part of the plant a painful swelling
of the throat may cause inadequate breathing.

EUROPEAN BEECH, *Fagus sylvatica.* This is a
popular imported ornamental tree of the Beech
family which comes in many varieties. 3½-5
inch long alternate leaves are lustrous dark-green,
finely and somewhat remotely toothed and more
or less elliptic-ovate. Humans have been poisoned from ingesting the nut (beechnut) inside the
woody, prickly covering, for it can be easily
mistaken for the harmless American species.
The pollen may trigger hay fever.

FALSE HELLEBORE, INDIAN POKE, *Veratrum viride.* This is a perennial herb of the Lily family, commonly found in damp areas of eastern North America. *V. californicum* Durand (corn lily) is one of the most poisonous plants in the Sierra. Alternate, clasping leaves are 6-12 inches long, to 6 inches wide. The shape is oval with deeply cut veins which appear pleated. The entire plant, especially the roots, is toxic.

GOLDEN DEWDROP, PIGEONBERRY, SKY FLOWER DURANTA,*Duranta repens.* This drooping shrub to 18 feet tall of the Vervain family is cultivated in warm parts of the United States as an ornamental. 1-2 inch long leaves are ovalish, and coarsely-toothed. Stems are often thorny and trailing. The leaves are toxic, and eating the eight-seeded, yellow-orange berries has caused serious illness and death among children.

GOPHER PLANT, MOLE PLANT, *Euphorbia lathyrus.* Reputed to control gophers and moles, this biennial of the Spurge family grows on a single stem to 5 feet by the second summer. Leaves are mainly opposite, 1½-5 inches long, narrow, and pointed. A cluster of yellow flowers blooms at the top of the stem during the second year. The stems contain a poisonous milky sap which can irritate the skin, open cuts and eyes upon contact.

GROUNDSEL, RAGWORT,*Senecio spp.* There are about 50 poisonous species of this member of the Sunflower family, growing as a weed in pastures and meadows everywhere. Sometimes ragwort is used as a tall border plant in gardens. Stalked basal leaves are to 8 inches long, cut into lyre-shaped lobes. Stem leaves are broadly lance-shaped, to 6 inches long, and cut into 2-3 lobes. The poisonous parts are the stems and leaves which may cause severe liver damage when eaten in quantities.

HENBANE, BLACK HENBANE,*Hyoscyamus niger.* This is a coarse Nightshade family annual or biennial. It was first introduced as a medicinal herb and since naturalized, becoming common in the East and Northern Rockies. Erect hairy stems grow to 30 inches high. Alternate 5-7 inch long leaves are oblongish, and coarsely-toothed or lobed,with long hairs on the midrib. The alkaloids found in the seeds and juice are deadly poisonous, a fact known to ancient Egyptians.

HORSE BEAN, BROAD BEAN, FAVA BEAN, *Vicia Faba.* A strong-growing herb belonging to the Pea family, this annual is commonly grown throughout the United States to furnish food for humans and livestock. The erect, 5 foot high plant has alternate leaves, with 2-6 pairs of ovalish leaflets, each 2-4 inches long, without tendrils. Certain individuals upon eating the raw or half-cooked beans acquire a severe poisoning called *"favism".* Most of those affected are children. A genetic trait is believed to be involved. Inhaling the pollen from the flowers can cause dizziness and a headache within 2-3 hours.

HORSETAIL, *Equisetum arvense.* A small perennial herb of the Horsetail family, this weed grows in moist places throughout the United States. The hollow-stemmed, jointed, green plant has no true leaves nor does it bear flowers. Children have been poisoned from using the young green stems for blowguns and whistles. (Not illus.)

HYACINTH, *Hyacinthus orientalis.* A bulbous herb of the Lily family, this common garden or potted hyacinth has green leaves nearly 12 inches long and about ¾ of an inch wide, without marginal teeth. The poisonous principle is concentrated in the large bulb. Ingesting only a small amount of a hyacinth bulb may cause severe stomach upset.

INDIAN HEMP, DOGBANE, *Apocynum cannabinum.* A perennial milky-juiced herb of the Dogbane family, this weed is scattered throughout the United States in open fields, pastures, along roadsides and streams. Sometimes the plant is cultivated for ornament and for use in medicine. Opposite leaves are simple, near-

ly 5 inches long and about half as wide, with smooth margins. The entire plant is poisonous. The spreading rootstock produces vomiting and stomach disturbances when eaten.

INKWEED, DRYMARY, *Drymaria pachyphylla.* A tender, succulent herb of the Stonecrop family, this gray-green summer annual grows naturally in frost-free areas where the soil is alkaline clay, or else it is propagated in greenhouses. Opposite leaves are paired, obovate to ovate with a blunt tip, and less than ½ inch long by ¼ inch wide. A purplish juice can be squeezed from the unripened seed capsule, thus the name inkweed. All parts of the plant are highly toxic.

JACK-IN-THE-PULPIT, INDIAN TURNIP, *Arisaema triphyllum.* Arum family. Indians heated and ate the tuberous, very acrid roots, but if eaten raw they will cause a painful swelling of the mouth. Both leaves and roots may cause skin irritation on contact. (Not illus.)

KENTUCKY COFFEE TREE, *Gymnocladus dioica.* A large, rough-barked tree of the Pea family, it grows to 80 feet in moist woods from Canada south to Alabama, Oklahoma, and Tennessee. Occasionally the tree is cultivated. Twice-compound leaves are arranged feather-fashion in 3-7 pairs of leaflets which are more or less ovalish, without marginal teeth and 2-4 inches long. The fruit is a thick, flat pod, containing 4-7 flat broad seeds, with a sticky pulp between them. The leaves, seeds and pulp are dangerously poisonous if eaten.

LOBELIA, INDIAN TOBACCO, *Lobelia inflata.* An annual herb of the Lobelia family, Indian tobacco is so-called because Indians dried and smoked the leaves of the weed. This species of *Lobelia* is a native in waste areas, woodlands, and roadsides throughout eastern North America. Numerous other species occur in similar places elsewhere in this country. Leaves are alternate, simple, pointed, and sparingly wavy-toothed, the uppermost leaves very small, narrow and acute. The slightly hairy stem is branching. All parts of the plant contain a milky, very toxic juice and all species can cause human poisoning. Leaves, stems, and fruit are a frequent cause of dermatitis.

LOCOWEED, *Astragalus spp.* These vetch-like herbs of the Pea family are found over most of the world, not all of which are poisonous. Loco is one species of *Astragalus* long recognized as a dangerous plant. It is found in the Rocky Mountain states westward and south into Texas and Mexico. The leaves are pinnate with the leaflets arranged feather-fashion. The degree of toxicity depends upon the type of soil on which the plants grow.

MAIDENHAIR TREE, *Ginkgo biloba.* This is a deciduous Chinese tree, the only survivor of the Ginkgo family, and often planted along streets or in yards. The fan-shaped leaves resemble a single pinnule of a maidenhair fern. The fleshy yellow fruit of the female tree is not only ill-smelling, but contains contact poisons. (Not illus.)

MANROOT, WILD CUCUMBER, *Marah fabaceus* or *Echinocystis lobata.* Gourd family. The stems come from a root that may weigh 50 pounds. Juice from the bitter-tasting root is poisonous and the hard, round seeds inside the densely spiny fruit are sometimes toxic when swallowed. (Not illus.) Do not confuse with *Ipomoea pandurata*, known as manroot.

MARIJUANA, HEMP, HASHISH, *Cannabis sativa.* A 6-12 foot tall annual herb of the Mulberry family, this rough-stemmed weed is distributed throughout the United States. Cultivation is prohibited by federal and state laws unless a license is granted. Compound leaves are opposite below, and alternate above. 3-7 long, slender coarsely-toothed leaflets are arranged finger-fashion. Around the small green flowers of the female plant is found a sticky gum which provides the narcotic hashish. Chewing the green plant or smoking the dried leaves can cause injury to the nervous system. Changes in behavior patterns are helpful indicators of poisoning.

MARSH MARIGOLD, COWSLIP, *Caltha palustris.* A Crowfoot family perennial found in marshes or by brooks. 3-6 inch wide leaves are roundish, heart or kidney-shaped and entire. Young leaves and stems are especially toxic and may be fatal if eaten in large quantities. (Not illus.)

MAYAPPLE, MANDRAKE, *Podophyllum peltatum.* A perennial herb of the Barberry family, the mayapple grows in damp meadows, woodlands, pastures, and along roadsides throughout the United States. Umbrella-shaped leaves are almost 12 inches wide with 5-9 lobes. Although the creeping, fleshy rootstock is used in preparing medicine commercially, it is poisonous by contact. Children have been poisoned by eating the young green leaves and the unripened berries. The ripe fruit is edible.

MOONSEED, *Menispermum canadense.* This perennial, woody vine of the Moonseed family is a native of eastern North America, but is cultivated in other parts of the United States. Alternate leaves are 4-8 inches long. They are round to oval, sometimes lobed. The young leaves are softly-hairy beneath. Poisonous parts of the plant are the leaves and the bluish-black fruits

hanging in grape-like clusters. The difference is it has a single crescent-shaped seed per berry, while a grape contains many seeds.

MUSTARD, *Brassica nigra*. This is a Mustard family cultivated commercial plant as well as a familiar weed. All parts of the black mustard plants are toxic if eaten raw in large quantities. (Not illus.)

NIGHT-BLOOMING JESSAMINE, *Cestrum nocturnum*. This Nightshade family shrub is cultivated for its fragrant night-blooming, trumpet-shaped flowers. Alternate 2-3½ inch long,entire leaves are oblongish or oval. The fruit is small and berry-like. All cestrums are extremely poisonous if any part is eaten.

PASQUE FLOWER, *Anemone patens*. A perennial herb of the Crowfoot family, pasque flower is a native of the dry prairies of the Midwest, but is also cultivated in flower gardens. The 6 inch high plant has a flowering stalk about 12 inches in height. Long-stalked basal leaves are divided into three divisions. Each of these divisions is divided again into many narrow, fine segments. Purplish-blue flowers bloom before the leaves develop. The entire plant is toxic.

PAWPAW, *Asimina triloba*. This is a medium-sized tree of the Custard-Apple family. When ripe the banana-flavored, yellow flesh of the potato-shaped fruit often causes severe stomach pains if eaten raw. The entire plant is suspected of causing dermatitis. (Not illus.)

PHEASANT'S EYE, *Adonis vernalis*. A perennial herb of the Crowfoot family, this plant is a popular cultivated ornamental, especially in rock gardens. Plants grow about 9 inches high. Alternate leaves are crowded and finely-dissected, almost fern-like. It has a solitary yellow, 3 inch wide flower which consists of 5-15 petals. The flower center is dark and prominent. White and double-flowered varieties exist. Leaves and stems are toxic, and eating large quantities of the seeds may be fatal.

PITTOSPORUM, AUSTRALIAN LAUREL, *Pittosporum spp.* These evergreen shrubs and trees of the family Tobira consist of more than 100 species, several of which are cultivated in southern parts of the United States and especially in California. Alternate leaves on young trees are whorled, wavy-margined, and faintly-toothed or without teeth. The poisonous parts of the plants if ingested are the leaves, stems, and the reddish fruits with their capsules of sticky seeds.

POINSETTIA, *Euphorbia pulcherrima.* A popular Christmas season plant of the Spurge family, the colorful bracts clustered at the top are often mistaken for flowers. All parts of the plant contain a poisonous milky sap. In Texas a boy died after eating a single leaf. (Not illus.)

POISON SUMAC, *Rhus vernix.* This is a rangy Sumac family shrub or tree to 25 feet found growing in the swamps of eastern North America. It has compound leaves with 7-11 pointed leaflets without marginal teeth. Leaf and leaflet stalks are reddish. Clustered whitish fruits resemble poison ivy. The entire plant including the pollen contains very dangerous contact poisons.

RAGWEED, *Ambrosia spp.* Many species of ragweed are distributed throughout the United States. They appear in cultivated areas as well as wastelands and roadsides. *A. artemisiifolia* is typical. It is a coarse, roughish herb from 3-12 feet high with 3-5 lobed leaves. Numerous flowers are borne in tall, often branching, spike-like clusters. Upside down appearing flowerheads are turban-shaped. In the fall its abundant pollen, especially *A. trifida,* makes it one of the leading causes of hay fever, often producing very serious congestions. Sunflower family.

RATTLEBOX, COFFEEWEED, *Daubentonia punicea* or *Sesbania punicea.* This is a deciduous shrub or small tree of the Pea family to 12 feet high. It is planted for ornament but has become naturalized in the southeastern coastal states. Compound leaves with 12-40 leaflets are 4-8 inches long, each with a sharp tip and without marginal teeth. The fruit, a four-winged pod, is about 3 inches long and contains several toxic seeds. Leaves and showy pea-like red, orange, or scarlet flowers are also poisonous when eaten. Remove and destroy developing pods.

RUBBERVINE, *Cryptostegia grandiflora.* A tropical woody vine of the Milkweed family, so-named because it yields rubber but not commercially. It is grown for ornament indoors northward and cultivated in gardens in the south. Opposite 3-4 inch long leaves are oblongish, thick, glossy and without marginal teeth. Leaves and stems contain a milky juice. Flowers are funnel-shaped and purplish. The fruit is an angle-shaped pod. All parts may cause serious stomach and intestinal upset.

ST. JOHNS-WORT, KLAMATH WEED, *Hypericum perforatum.* This species of the colorful St. Johns-wort family has become naturalized as a weed throughout most of the United States. An erect perennial herb, the opposite, stalkless entire leaves are oblong, ½-1 inch long, resinous-dotted. Stems and branches are two-edged or winged. Yellow flowers are five-petaled and 3-5 to a cluster. The fruit is a capsule. All parts of the plant are poisonous when eaten and cultivated species of *Hypericum* are suspected of being toxic, too.

SCARLET PIMPERNEL, *Anagallis arvensis.* This Primrose family almost prostrate annual herb is found growing as a tiny, attractive weed in the Middle Atlantic and Pacific Coast states. Opposite, entire leaves are oval-shaped. Small, pale scarlet bell-shaped flowers close at the approach of bad weather. The poisonous properties in this plant have long been recognized. The leaves may cause an irritation to the skin.

SCOTCH BROOM, *Cytisus scoparius.* This is a tall, brushy, stiffly-branched shrub of the Pea family that grows to 9 feet high. Broom has spread like a weed over open lands in California and the Northwest, and along the East Coast south to Georgia. More handsome varieties are popular in gardens. The plant has compound leaves with three leaflets which are 1/3-1/2 inches long each, but these are sometimes reduced to a single leaflet. The pea-like flowers are bright yellow. Seeds in the flat, pea-like pod are the poisonous part of the plant.

SNOWDROP, *Galanthus nivalis.* This is an Amaryllis family bulbous herb, prized by gardeners for its early blooming flowers. The small bulbs containing alkaloids, may cause stomach and intestinal upset. (Not illus.)

SORGHUM, *Sorghum vulgare.* These commercially cultivated coarse annual grasses include saccharin or forage sorghums, grain sorghums, and broom corn. Their pithy stems reach to 15 feet, their height depending on the variety and growing conditions. The seed is borne in heads of loose branches or panicles sometimes 8 inches thick, and more than a foot long. A very dangerous toxic liquid is present in the plants. The broad young leaves have the highest content of this poison. If eaten in large amounts, there is a risk of prussic acid poisoning. Grass family.

SPANISH BAYONET, *Yucca aloifolia.* An evergreen perennial of the Agave family, this species of yucca is widely grown in gardens throughout the southwestern part of the United States. It is a plant of many uses. The poisonous part is centered in the roots. (Not illus.)

SPIDER LILY, *Hymenocallis americana.* This bulbous herb of the Amaryllis family grows naturally from South Carolina to Florida but is also cultivated in gardens. It has narrow, strap-shaped, basal leaves, with a few-flowered cluster of white flowers at the end of a stout, solid, flattened stem or scape. The poisonous part of the plant is the bulb which grows larger as it ages.

SPINDLE TREE, *Euonymus europaeus.* A shrub or small tree 9-20 feet high of the Staff-tree family, this plant is grown in yards but has sometimes escaped cultivation. The opposite, stalked, deciduous leaves are oblongish, 1½-4 inch long, wavy-toothed, and wedge-shaped at the bases. Flowers are yellowish-green. The fruit is four-lobed, red or pink, with an orange aril. Leaves, bark, and fruit cause severe diarrhea and are dangerous to children when eaten.

STAR-OF-BETHLEHEM, *Ornithogalum umbellatum.* This bulbous herb of the Lily family is common in American gardens and has become naturalized as a weed in eastern North America. Bulbs are onion-like, 1 inch thick. Basal, 6-12 inch long leaves are ¼-½ inch wide and veined or spotted white. The leafless stem or scape is 6-8 inches long. 12-20 star-like flowers in a cluster are white, the 3 outer segments having green margins. All parts contain colchicine and are toxic.

SWEET PEA, *Lathyrus odoratus.* A common very fragrant annual vine of the Pea family, it is cultivated in many varieties everywhere. Regular consumption of the seeds can cause bone deformaties and paralysis of legs and arms. Wild sweet pea seeds have also proven to be poisonous. (Not illus.)

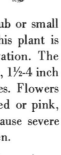

TANSY, *Tanacetum vulgare.* A strong-scented herb of the Sunflower family, the rather weedy plant, 2-3 feet high, is often used in herb gardening, but has become naturalized throughout North America. Tansy has a perennial creeping root. Alternate leaves are much dissected and a dark-green. Flowers are a golden-yellow. The foliage is poisonous when eaten in quantities.

TRILLIUM, WAKEROBIN, *Trillium spp.* There are about thirty species of this beautiful perennial herb belonging to the Lily family growing throughout the United States, either in woodlands or else cultivated in gardens. Each spring the flowering stalks arise from thick, short, rootstocks. Scale-like sheathing leaves appear at the base. The three real leaves are arranged in a whorl near the top of the stalk. These leaves are simple, ovalish, smooth and parallel-veined. Eating the toxic rootstocks produces violent vomiting.

TRUMPET-CREEPER, COWITCH, *Campsis radicans.* A woody, high-climbing vine of the Trumpet-creeper family, this hardy plant is a native of the woods in eastern United States, but is often planted in gardens elsewhere. Compound leaves are divided into 9-11 ovate leaflets, 2½ inches long, with marginal teeth. Flowers that grow in a cluster are 3 inch long, orange tubes with flaring scarlet lobes. The fruit is a long pod with a many-winged seed. Leaves and flowers are one of the most common causes of dermatitis.

VIRGINIA CREEPER, *Parthenocissus quinquefolia.* A member of the Grape family, this common woody vine grows naturally in woods, fields, and disturbed areas throughout the eastern United States. The vigorous vine is cultivated in gardens everywhere. There is also a western wild species *(P. vitacea).* Alternate leaves are long-stalked and divided into five separate, 6 inch leaflets. The leaflets are oval, but pointed toward the rounded ends and toothed on the margins. Eating the small, almost black berries has caused poisoning and death of children.

WALNUT, *Juglans spp.* Several species of these tall, deciduous trees of the Walnut family are cultivated throughout the United States. The outer green hulls of the nuts in all species contain a poisonous juice which often causes a severe skin irritation on contact. (Not illus.)

WATER HEMLOCK, *Cicuta maculata.* This 3-7 foot tall perennial herb of the Carrot family is found on edges of ponds and in bogs throughout eastern North America. All parts of the plant are dangerously poisonous, especially the short, tuberous bundle of roots. Children have been poisoned by using the stems for blowguns and whistles. (Not illus.)

WILD ONION, *Allium canadense* or *Allium cernuum.*
A bulbous herb of the Amaryllis family, this species is
found in meadows and woodlands in the northeastern
and north-central states. Other wild species grow
throughout the western United States. Leaves are
narrow, long, and with parallel edges, arising from the
small bulb. All parts of the plant are poisonous when
eaten in great quantities, especially if they have started
to decay. Cultivated onions *(A. Cepa)* contain the same toxic principle.

WILD RED CHERRY, PIN CHERRY, *Prunus
pensylvanica.* This is a native deciduous tree,
sometimes shrubby to 30 feet high, of the Rose
family, and common throughout most of North
America. Alternate 3-5½ inch long leaves are
oblongish or lance-oblong, and sharply but finely-toothed, the tip elongated. The entire plant
is poisonous, especially wilted leaves, bark and
pits. The red fruit is safe to eat if the pits are
removed. Poisoning of children has resulted from making *"tea"* out of
the leaves. Wild black cherry *(P. serotina)* and cultivated cherries are
similarly poisonous as all contain prussic acid.

WISTERIA, *Wisteria spp.* This is a very showy, fragrant, popular woody vine or small tree of the Pea
family. Various species are cultivated over most of
the United States. Alternate leaves are compound,
the leaflets arranged feather-fashion, with an odd one
at the end. The pea-like flowers, of a variety of colors,
hang in long clusters. Eating the flattened, pea-like
pods and the seeds cause stomach and intestinal upset. One or two seeds
are enough to make a child seriously ill.

WORMSEED, MEXICAN TEA, *Chenopodium am-
brosioides.* Considered to be the strongest smelling of
all weeds, this sometimes annual herb of the Goose-
foot family is commonly found in gardens everywhere.
Alternate, nearly stalkless, leaves have a slightly toothed and undulating margin. Numerous, tiny greenish
flowers are borne in a terminal leafy cluster. The
seeds contain dangerous oils and are the source of
poisoning. Dig out plants before seeds set to be safe.

REFERENCES

PAMPHLETS—Write to your nearest State University, Agricultural Extension Service for pamphlets on poisonous plants usually mailed for a nominal price. Another source is the Superintendent of Documents, Government Printing Office, Washington, D.C., 20402, asking for the list of publications on poisonous plants.

Wild food field trips, films, talks and demonstrations are recommended to be added to what is read. If possible, visit the W.C. Muenscher Poisonous Plants Garden in New York State Veterinary College, Ithaca, New York. More than 100 varieties of toxic plants are on display. Dr. John Kingsbury, a well-known authority on poisonous plants, is in charge of this exhibit.

IDENTIFYING SPECIMENS—Such local sources of information as Poison Control Centers will help you identify specimens. However, New York State College of Agriculture offers a mail-order service to identify plants for people with no local means of help. Packaged plants may be sent to Extension Specialist, D.H. Bailey Hortorium, Ithaca, New York, 14850 with an accompanying letter explaining exactly where the plant was found and the date it was collected.

References especially good for additional study and valuable help with better identification of poisonous plants are listed below.

Bailey, L.H., *Manual of Cultivated Plants*, Revised Edition, Macmillan Company, New York, 1949, 1971.

Dreisbach, Robert H., *Handbook of Poisoning*, Lange Medical Publications, Los Altos, California, 1971.

Fernald, Merritt Lyndon, Alfred Charles Kinsey, and Reed C. Rollins, *Edible Wild Plants of Eastern North America*, Revised, Harper & Row, New York, 1958.

Hardin, James W. and Arena, Jay M., M.D., *Human Poisoning from Native and Cultivated Plants*, Duke University Press, Durham, N.C., 1969.

Kingsbury, John M., *Deadly Harvest*, Holt, Rinehart & Winston, New York, 1965.

Kingsbury, John M., *Poisonous Plants of the United States and Canada*, Prentice-Hall, Englewood Cliffs, New Jersey, 1964.

Muenscher, W.C., *Poisonous Plants of the United States*, Revised, Macmillan Co., New York, 1951, 1970.

Munz, Philip A., *A California Flora*, University of California Press, 1963.

Sunset Western Garden Book, Lane Magazine and Book Co., Menlo Park, California, 1967.

Taylor, Norman, *Taylor's Encyclopedia of Gardening*, Fourth Edition, Houghton, Mifflin Co., Boston, Massachusetts, 1961.

Tucker, John M., Kimball, M.H., *Poisonous Plants in the Garden*, 1966, (AXT-22 pamphlet) Univ. Ex. Service, 229 Univ. Hall, Berkeley, Ca.

GLOSSARY

Achene: A small, dry one-seeded fruit.

Alternate: Leaf arrangement other than opposite or whorled.

Annual: A plant which germinates, grows, flowers, has fruit and dies within a single year.

Aril: A process adhering to a part of the seed.

Axil: An (upper) angle formed by a leaf or branch with the stem.

Base: The part of the plant nearest the point of attachment.

Berry: A many-seeded fleshy fruit.

Biennial: A plant requiring two growing seasons from seed to maturity and death.

Blade: The expanded, broad and flattened part of a leaf.

Bracts: Leaf-like organs usually confined to the stalk of a flower, or just beneath the flower itself.

Branchlet: The growth of last season on a stem or branch.

Bulb: An underground bud from which certain plants grow.

Bulbous: Growing from bulbs.

Capsule: A dry fruit that splits along two or more lines and has more than one row of seeds.

Cluster: The arrangement of flowers in a group.

Coma: A condition of not being able to feel, think, or notice.

Compound: Having more than one separate leaflet to a leafstalk.

Convulsion: A violent uncontrollable series of contracting muscles.

Corm: A short bulb-like underground stem, but lacking scales.

Deciduous: Leaves which drop off in the autumn.

Dermatitis: A skin infection caused by a plant. The severity of poisoning depends on the plant contacted, the degree of contact, and the sensitiveness of the person involved.

Entire: Pertaining to the margin, not toothed.

Erect: A plant or its part standing upright.

Evergreen: Leaves which remain green throughout the year.

Flower: The blossom of a plant; the part that comprises the reproductive organs and their cover.

Foliage: The leaves on a plant, collectively.

Fruit: The ripened ovary of a plant with all its accessory parts.

Gills: The part under the cap of a mushroom that bears the spores.

Hairy: With fairly long hairs.

Herb: A plant without a woody stem.

Husk: The outer shell or covering of any fruit.

Leaflet: A segment of a compound leaf.

Lobe: A division of a leaf whose margin is deeply cut.

Margin: The border or edge of a leaf; when it is entire it is smooth.

Narcotic: A drug that produces an insensible condition, or lessens pain by dulling the nerves.

Naturalized: Introduced originally from a foreign area and growing and reproducing without cultivation.

Nerve: The simple vein of a leaf or slender rib.

Nut: A hard, mostly one-seeded fruit.

Oblong: A leaf that is longer than wide with nearly parallel sides.

Obovate: Inversely ovate.

Opposite: Two leaves at a node, against each other.

Oval: A leaf less than twice as long as wide.

Ovate: Like a hens egg, the broad end downward, at the base.

Parasite: A plant living in, on, or with another living host organism.

Perennial: A plant lasting year after year.

Petal: One of the usually colored leaves forming the inner circle of leaf-like parts of a flower, next to and surrounding the stamens.

Pinnate: A compound leaf arranged feather-like.

Pinnule: A division of a pinna (primary division of a compound leaf).

Pod: Any dry fruit that splits open, as a pea pod.

Pollen: A powder needed in fertilization and usually yellow, discharged from the enlarged tips of the **stamens** (or male parts) of a flower.

Respiratory: Relating to the lungs and other breathing organs.

Rhizome: An underground stem, often thick and horizontal, producing leafy shoots on the upper sides and roots below.

Rib: The primary vein or nerve in a leaf.

Rootstock: A rhizome or source of stems and roots; in general any root system.

Scape: A leafless stem rising from the ground.

Seed: The part from which a flower, vegetable, or other plant grows into a new plant. Ripened ovule.

Shoot: The young stem and leaves of a plant.

Shrub: A woody plant, branched from the base, usually less than 15 feet tall.

Simple: A leaf not branched.

Spasm: An unnatural, uncontrolled muscular contraction.

Species: A group of individual plants having common characteristics.

Spike: A cluster of stalkless flowers borne close together on an elongated stem.

Spore: A single cell capable of growing into a new plant.

Spur: A tubular, hollow-pointed process in certain flowers, and ordinarily secreting nectar.

Stalk: The stem-like structure at the base of a flower or leaf.

Stupor: Partial or complete unconsciousness.

Thorn: A fairly long, hard, sharp-pointed plant structure (a modified branch).

Toothed: Small projections or lobes on the margin of a leaf.

Tremor: An involuntary shaking, trembling, or shivering.

Tuber: A swollen, mostly underground stem which bears many buds as in the potato.

Variety: A group of plants within a species.

Veins: Strands of tissue forming the framework of leaves.

Woolly: Covered with long, tangled, soft hairs.

INDEX